EMPOWERING
the One in Eight

Copyright © 2024 Ify Oji

The moral rights of the author have been asserted.

Apart from any fair dealing for the purposes of research or private study, or criticism or re-view, as permitted under Copyright, Design and Patents Act 1998, this publication may only be reproduced, stored or transmitted, in any form or by any means, with prior permission in writing of the publishers, or in any case of the reprographic reproduction in accordance with the terms of licences issued by the Copyright Licensing Agency. Enquiries concerning reproduction outside these terms should be sent to the publishers.

PublishU Ltd.

www.PublishU.com

All rights of this publication are reserved.

Thank You

I am profoundly grateful to my family for their endless love and encouragement, especially during the intense late nights and early mornings spent writing this book. Thank you to my friend, Yinka Sokunbi, who encouraged me to register for a book writing class which would eventually kick-start my journey to publishing. To my support network of friends – thank you for your unwavering support, understanding and belief in my ability.

A heartful thank you to my husband, Solomon Oji, whose guidance and constructive criticism helped shape this manuscript into its final form. Your expertise was invaluable. Thank you to my children for understanding why Mummy was constantly in the study and writing.

Special appreciation to Matt Bird and PublishU for their exceptional design and layout skills which have transformed my words into a visually captivating book. To my readers – thank you for investing your time and attention in these pages. Your curiosity and engagement mean the world to me.

Lastly, thank you to those who offered encouragement and inspiration along the way. Your kindness and generosity have not gone unnoticed.

I dedicate this book to the memory of my Uncle John Okoye and my friend Temitope Adeosun, both of whom courageously fought in the battle against cancer and are dearly missed. May their souls continue to rest in perfect peace.

For those still in the fight: Every day you face challenges that would test the strongest among us, yet you continue to fight with unwavering courage and resilience. Remember, in your journey, you're not alone. Each step forward, no matter how small, is a testament to your incredible strength and determination. Keep believing in yourself, keep leaning on your support system and keep holding onto hope. Your bravery inspires us all and together, we stand with you in the fight.

With sincere gratitude,

Ify Oji

Content

Introduction: The Unseen Hand

Chapter 1: Concept of Being 1 in 8

Chapter 2: The Emotional Impact of a Life-Altering Diagnosis: Navigating the Depths of Uncertainty

Chapter 3: The Role of Faith in Coping with a Diagnosis

>Clinging to Faith in Healing

>Shaken by Trials but not Stirred

>Where is God in All of This?

>Practicing Self-Compassion in the Face of of Adversity

>Create a Quiet Space

Chapter 4: The Necessity of Trials in the Journey of a Believer

>Introduction

>The Purpose of Trials in Spiritual Growth

>Trials as a Path to Deeper Understanding

>Trials as Tests of Faith

>Trials as a Catalyst for Empathy & Compassion

>Trials as Catalysts for Personal Transformation

>The Role of Faith in Navigating Trials

Chapter 5: The Significance of Friendship During Difficult Times: A Personal Journey

Chapter 6: Setbacks and Triumphs

Faith

Chapter 7: Providing Essential Support

Chapter 8: Confronting Your Fears

Rising Strong: Finding Strength and Empowerment Through Life's Challenges

The Power of Praise and Worship

Chapter 9: Christian Perspectives on Trials

Confronting Your Fears: A Journey to Personal Empowerment

The Spectrum of Emotions

The Challenges of Post-Diagnosis Fear

Chapter 10: Navigating Breast Cancer Treatment and Lifestyle Changes

Introduction

Understanding Your Breast Cancer Treatment Plan

Building a Support System

Adopting Healthy Lifestyle Changes

Coping with Lifestyle Changes

Setting Realistic Goals

Embracing a Positive Mindset

Chapter 11: Conclusion

Summary

Sources

About the Author

EMPOWERING THE ONE IN EIGHT

Introduction
The Unseen Hand

At the ripe age of thirty-seven, I found myself reflecting on the patchwork quilt that was my life. Each square represents experiences lived, challenges overcome, and blessings received: all woven together by threads of unending grace. Life had indeed treated me kindly. I was blessed with a robust bill of health, only modestly marred by the stubborn pounds that clung to me, souvenirs of motherhood's profound journey. But even they were no match for my spirit; I pursued fitness with vigour, making sure I kept up with my daily walks.

Motherhood, they say, is a dance of endurance and delicate balance. I danced it well, steering clear of hospital corridors, save for the joyous occasions that brought my children into the world. In my family's life, grace was as tangible as the morning dew, and our needs – from the mundane to the profound – were met with the assurance that God's hand was evident in our lives. We dwelt in a constant state of sufficiency, a testament to the faith that pulsed at the heart of our existence.

Relocating to the Middle East tested the fabric of that faith. My eldest, barely three and with speech delays and not able to communicate, became the focus of our fervent prayers and practical efforts. Solomon and I poured our essence into nurturing him, a dedication matched only by the relentless chatter of his twin siblings, whose daily babble-filled exuberance proved to be a divine form of intervention. Then, like a miracle couched in an ordinary moment, reading to my silent son awakened his voice – a voice that chose to reveal itself through the written word before blossoming into speech. A house brimming with small miracles became our normal, each new day unravelling the goodness of the Lord in our lives.

It was during this time of acclimation to new norms and cultures that providence shone through once again in my professional journey. Amidst the new environment and new norms, I scarcely dared to hope for swift employment. Yet, the unexpected came to pass – a job materialised within the first few months of our arrival. Our dreams, cloaked in the cautious fabric of a five-year plan, were suddenly reimagined and amplified. The land we came to explore embraced us and before we knew it, the five years were a mere prologue to a longer, richer chapter borne of the land's munificence. Through every moment, God's faithfulness remained our cornerstone, unshaken and resolute.

My mind, ever so often, would meander through the hallways of memories, lingering at the doorstep of my childhood. The boarding school years were now distant echoes, a time when we learned to tread confidently on the stepping stones of trust and faith. That same trust became the compass that guided us through life's tapestry, ever steering us towards gratitude, the compass that taught us to persist through adversity.

Navigating life with faith was akin to sailing on a sea with mercurial moods – sometimes calm, sometimes tempestuous. In our voyage, bold declarations of faith echoed against waves of challenge, mingling with whispered wisdom when quiet tact was needed. We became intentional actors in our journey, imbibing life's essence not in solitude but in the sacred fellowship of the community. By engaging with others who navigated their storied paths, we found strength, solace and the shared music of collective endurance. Here, amid the throngs of shared experiences, we propped each other up, finding joy in the whisper of encouragement, the grasp of a helping hand, and the undeniable presence of the Unseen Hand guiding us all.

EMPOWERING THE ONE IN EIGHT

Chapter 1
Concept of Being 1 in 8

Life has been great. I had only been in Saudi Arabia for about eight years at the time. We had just survived a pandemic, and I had been working full-time at the hospital, since moving from the United Kingdom after my husband got a job in the Middle East. We settled down to life. It had been a wonderful experience so far, but life was a lot slower. We had so much family time and were able to take the kids to whatever activities they were interested in.

Moving to Saudi Arabia remains one of the best decisions of my life. The only downside is that they are sceptical of working part-time. I remember being offered the job as a midwife although I was really after a public health job when I spoke to Human Resources (HR) and told them I was only interested in working three times a week as the kids were still under three. The HR representative looked puzzled. He couldn't believe what I was asking for. He gazed at my forehead avoiding any eye contact whatsoever and said to me, "We don't work part-time. You will work forty hours a week." I couldn't believe it. I had just moved from working fifteen hours a week in the UK and here I was about to commit to working more hours. I quickly called Solomon and told him, and he responded that I had no choice but that we will find out ways to make it work.

So eight years down the line, I had been working full time including working night shifts (which I hated doing), and here you had to commit to at least working five nights a month. Nights were my worst nightmare. I remember always having to swap my shifts with colleagues who loved working night shifts. I always found it difficult to sleep during the day, I would come back from work, have a shower and something to eat and then eventually fall asleep around 10 am and wake up around three or four o'clock. I was always tired and I constantly had black eye bags. But somehow, I managed it for at least eight years. My health was great, my only issue was trying to lose the baby weight. My weight was between eight-five to ninety kilograms. I loved walking and would spend most of my day off at the gym. At one point I had a fitness instructor. I did lose the weight but put it back on after a few months. We cherished the slower pace of life, relishing family time and indulging our children's interests.

The pandemic came and went and by God's grace, we survived it. During that season shortly after, I noticed that I just wanted to be by myself. I spent most of my days off watching sermons, studying the Bible – I wasn't interested in hanging out. The isolation from the pandemic also added to this new way of life (or so I thought). Thankfully, our hospital was well-equipped and as soon as the pandemic occurred, we went straight into protection and preservation mode. The Arabs don't joke when it comes to having the latest technical gadgets and protective equipment. Our hospital was well-equipped. I remember at one point we were helping other hospitals with equipment.

I recall on this particular night shift; it wasn't so busy most of the midwives were gathered at the nurse's station just talking about life, as we did most times when the unit was less busy. Amongst the nurses was one of my favourite obstetric doctors – very small in stature, always upbeat and never missed a moment to encourage. She was always happy and full of life. We spoke about random things that night and soon enough the conversation changed to checkups and blood tests. That was Dr Jan for you: She never missed a chance to remind you of your upcoming appointment or blood test or screening. I remember she was talking about a friend or so who lived in the United States of America and was going through some kind of treatment. As soon as that conversation ended, she quickly turned to me and said, "Ify, have you had your mammogram?" I laughed and reminded her that I wasn't forty yet and besides that, I was generally well – except for some pains I get during my period or just before I have it. She insisted that she would go ahead and book an Ultra Sound Scan (USS). I was shocked that one could have a USS in place of a mammogram. I couldn't argue. I told her I would go down to the department and try to get an appointment; she told me she would put in the request on the system and that I would be called for an appointment.

Two weeks later when I was back on day duty, I went to the USS department, and the lady said I could come down in a few hours to have it done on that day. I remember sitting there waiting to be called and feeling a bit anxious. I quickly brushed it aside. I generally always feel anxious as a patient – funny right? – being that I work in health care. My name was called, I went in and the sonographer greeted me and asked me how she could help because there was no real reason why I was there. I was too young to be having a scan, so I thought. I told her I was feeling some aches in my left breast. So I got ready for the USS, laid down and the lady started on the right breast, she went back and forth with the scan all through, and then I heard an echo but didn't think anything of it. Then she went to the left when she was done, she said she was going to repeat the scan on the right breast, my eyebrows were raised and I thought to myself, "Why will you want to repeat it?" As she continued with the scan I heard an echo, I didn't think anything of it. When she was done, she told me that I would get the report after the doctor's review. I said thank you, cleaned after myself, got dressed and returned to work. I had just arrived at my unit when my phone rang via Facebook Messenger. I looked and it was Dr Jan. She had gotten the report and said that they had found something. She quickly backed that statement up saying it is inconclusive and they are not sure what it is and are suggesting to re-scan me in six months. "I have referred you to be seen by the breast surgeon." I got off the phone and realised I was having palpitations. I had to sit down to get my thoughts together. A few minutes later I had a beep on my phone and it was the report of the USS stating that a mass measuring fifteen millimetres had been found. I read that report a couple of times throughout the day. At lunchtime that day another doctor called to say an appointment with the breast surgeon had been scheduled for two weeks. The day got busy. I went ahead to deliver two babies in that shift and I didn't have time to dwell on the report. When I got home after the shift I just prayed about it and kept the information to myself. I wasn't up to talking about it with anyone.

I remember telling Solomon a day after the USS and the report we prayed about it and left it at that. So on the day of the appointment with the breast surgeon, I remember

Solomon accompanied me to the doctor's office, and the doctor looked up at me and asked why I was there. I went ahead to explain my situation. He quickly brushed away my concerns saying it was probably nothing as I was young and had no history of breast cancer in my family. I remember telling him I wanted to have a biopsy of the mass, he looked shocked and said to me that he didn't see why I should have one, that there was no need for it; that I was better off coming back in six months for a breast ultrasound. I gave him a brief history of my background, I had worked several years in the healthcare profession and reminded him of the profession where I currently work, and how knowledgeable I was and well-informed about the choices that I wanted. So seeing that he could not win, he gave in and told me that he would speak to the breast clinic department and that they would contact me with an appointment.

As I waited for the appointment date, I reflected on the pandemic when I joined a prayer platform called New Season Prophetic Prayers and Declarations (NSPPD). The platform on social media was run by Pastor Jerry Eze. I recall logging in online one morning and glued into the session that day and during the prayer session, the pastor said to pray for each part of your body from your head to the soles of your feet that God will reveal to you anything that will cost you anything in future. So I started praying as the Holy Spirit led that morning. I prayed as I had never done before, so during this period of waiting I was reminded of the one I serve that He had perfected all that concerns me and that testimony will surely come out of this.

I got an appointment for my biopsy a few days later. It was scheduled for October. I looked at the date and it was our wedding anniversary, so I thought it was time to tell someone in my family. I remember calling my mum and telling her that I had to have a biopsy and the story leading up to that point. So my mum prayed and promised to continue to pray until the day of the biopsy.

The day arrived. Solomon took time off work to accompany me, the kids went off to school, we arrived at the hospital very early, and we sat down to wait for our allocated time slot. Solomon tried to reassure me he could tell I was very nervous; I didn't know what to think I was very scared. I saw people come and go; I could read their facial expressions, I wanted to know what they were thinking after their scan then it was time. I heard my name, then I heard the words, "Your husband won't be able to come in with you." Then I froze. I knew I was alone in this journey. I got into the room, and the support worker got me to change, she told me what was going to happen and what to expect, and then the sonographer came in again and told me she was going to do another scan to find the mass and then the doctor will come in to take a biopsy. I had been praying that the mass would not be found and that it would disappear, but at last, she found it and it was sitting pretty at the same place. So the doctor came in and the process started. As a healthcare professional, I was used to giving injections and watching epidural and spinal procedures and had never seen a needle as long as that, and as it pierced through my skin, I whispered, "Lord, take over. You know the end from the beginning and all the in-between. I lay it all at Your feet: all that I feel at this moment; my anxieties, my worries, this whole thing. Lord, take over." As I looked up at the screen, I could see the small mass. As the needle took samples, I could see it slowly disappear and then she left a clip inside to note the area the mass was taken from. The area was cleaned up and a tiny bandage was applied. It was pain-free and I had no aches except mentally.

As I walked out to meet Solomon, all I wanted to do was cry. I couldn't believe I was back again worrying about my health. And at that moment I had a flashback to 2013 just before I got pregnant with the twins. My cervical test results had come back abnormal, it was CIN 3 which was seen as worrying, and of course, there was nothing anyone could do as I was pregnant at the time. I was also going through a high-risk pregnancy as the doctors were worried that one twin was smaller than the other by two weeks, and they couldn't understand why at the time. It ended up being that I had conceived them two weeks apart which is very rare. This rare process is called superfetation. They were technically twins but they were also two different conceptions. Six weeks after I had the twins, I was back in hospital for a cervical biopsy which thankfully was negative and all my cervical swabs since that time have all been negative. So I took courage in the fact that the "I am, that I am" who has been my shield since then, is the same God today and I will continue to testify of His goodness. A Bible passage came to mind from 2 Corinthians 4:8-9,

"We are hard pressed on every side, but not crushed: perplexed, but not in despair, persecuted but not abandoned, struck down but not destroyed."

So Solomon looked at me and suggested we go out for breakfast. As we drove to the restaurant, it was silent because I was processing and my mind was a battlefield. We sat down to eat and all I could see was breast cancer awareness, the table mats, the decoration – everything was focused on breast cancer. At that point, I knew it was not going to be good news.

I forced myself to eat what I could and we went back home and tried to take my mind off it all. I was back to work the following day on the night shift. On the third day after the biopsy, having been a healthcare professional for so many years I knew that the results would be out. So I got to work that night. Luckily I was assigned to the assessment unit and at that time I had no patient, so I logged into my hospital chart and there in front of me was the result of the biopsy. At this point, I could feel my heart pounding at two hundred beats per minute and I could hear myself saying "Focus." All I could see at this point was Carcinoma. I became sweaty, I felt I was going to pass out, then I quickly took a screenshot of the result and shut down the computer. I couldn't believe it. I was shaking all over and before I knew what was happening, the tears began to fall down my face. I knew I couldn't continue with the shift even though I was only fifteen minutes into it, so I wiped my face and went searching for the midwife in charge of the shift and told her I couldn't continue and needed to go home. So she kept on asking why. Then I told her and I couldn't put the words together but she got the message. I quickly left before I was confronted by someone else. I got to the car park and began wailing, I looked up to the heavens and asked, "God, why? Why me? What did I do to deserve this?" I couldn't understand what was happening. For a minute, I thought I was dreaming and soon I would wake up from this bad dream. My heart kept pounding, so I picked up the courage and drove home. As I got into the house, Solomon was still in the living room, and seeing me he knew it wasn't good news. I told him we had to go to the park so as not to frighten the kids. We got to the park and I let out the biggest scream of my life. I wailed and wailed. All I could see was doom, that was it. I couldn't think beyond the one word from the report. Oh my kids! Who will look after them? I only got a few years and that's it. I cried and cried. I couldn't stop sobbing. I knew Solomon was talking but I didn't hear a word he said. I was lost in my emotions. I just wanted all of it to stop, but I couldn't because this right here was my reality.

When I finally got my heartbeat down to normal, I could finally make out what he said. All I could hear was, "I am here! We will fight this." I remember we were still at the pack and I wondered what the neighbours would think. So we finally made it back into the house, we went straight upstairs and prayed and cried and prayed and cried, and then I remembered I had a brother who was a doctor and not just any doctor, but a paediatric oncologist so I called him and told him the whole story and sent him a screenshot of the biopsy report. He screamed, prayed and then he was like, "Hold on, the report is not all bad. I think we have to be thanking God here." "What? I have cancer." He agreed that they found some cancerous cells however it was still early stage. Ductal Carcinoma Insitu (DCIS) means it is still in the duct and has not gone anywhere, and as I listened it all started coming together: the journey to that stage and how God had aligned everything. Indeed, what the enemy meant for evil, God had turned around for my good. The prayers, my life in general: He remains faithful. Here was God protecting me and making sure that all crooked parts were being made straight.

As the days went by, I waited for an official appointment with the doctor to discuss follow-up actions. Isaiah 41:10 reminded me of the God I serve who has instructed us to "fear not, for I am with thee. Be not dismayed for I am thy God. I will strengthen thee, yea I will help thee and uphold thee with the right hand of My righteousness."

Proverbs 3:5-6, "Trust in the Lord with all thy heart and lean not on your understanding, in all thy ways acknowledge Him and He will direct thy path."

So, I let go of all my worries, and my fears, I put them all at His feet. The tears kept flowing and I couldn't control my emotions. My eyes were constantly swollen, and I would look at the kids and run to the bathroom to cry. Every single day came with a different mood. I was no longer interested in speaking to anybody. I just wanted to be left alone in my thoughts. Two days later I had to travel to the United Kingdom and my mum happened to be around, so I thought about how I was going to break the news to her. I was not sure how she was going to react to it, so I went ahead to let her know that the result of the biopsy was out and it was cancer. I saw my mum trying to be strong but deep inside I could tell she was broken. She tried to do what any mother would do at that time: she encouraged me, prayed with me and thanked God that it was found early. And we both decided that I would have to tell my dad and my siblings.

My dad's reaction did surprise me. My dad is a man of faith who sees God in everything. The first thing he said to me was, "Why are you panicking? Don't you know your

God? Speak to Him and put your faith in action." You see, I grew up in a praying household. My parents were believers who made it their responsibility that we knew Christ at a young age. I have childhood memories of stamping Gideon Bibles every weekend, still proud when I come across Bibles in the hotel rooms. The first thing I do is to look inside and check if it has a stamp. The stamps have an address and location of the countries sponsoring the Bible. Even before I spoke to my dad, I already had a different mindset that God was turning all this around for my good.

Looking at some biblical examples of people who were faced with devastating news, the story of Job always comes to mind. Job was a prominent man who dealt with a series of unfortunate incidents. His story is a powerful example of perseverance in the face of adversity. He lost most of his livelihood, his stocks, his servants and ten of his children. He was also affected with painful sores while grieving. Irrespective of all he was going through, Job did not curse God; rather, he shaved his head, fell to his knees and worshipped God. He asked God for an explanation – of why all these mishaps were happening to him. God spoke to him reminding him of His sovereignty, wisdom and the complexity of creation and that there are mysteries beyond human understanding.

This encounter left Job with a deeper understanding of God. He repented of any arrogance he might have had in thinking he could understand God's way. In the end, God restored all that Job had lost and blessed him much more than before. Job's perseverance and unwavering faith even amid unimaginable suffering, serve as a powerful testament to strength and faith.

Most days I felt so isolated. During those days I reflected on my life just before the pandemic, I had spent most of my spare time by myself, and I was not interested in hanging out or calling anyone. I just felt the need to be still and to be by myself. Some days I studied my Bible, and some days I just lay in bed playing Gospel songs. I never fully understood why; it was not until my diagnosis that I began to put all the pieces together and I knew that God had started years in advance to prepare me for a time like this.

Jeremiah was a prophet in the Old Testament of the Bible who had a difficult and challenging ministry. He kept his faith despite all the numerous adversities he faced. His ministry began during a difficult period in Israel's history. God called him to prophesy during the reign of King Josiah and he also prophesied during the reign of several subsequent kings.

Jeremiah 1:4–10 tells us that he was reluctant to answer the call of God on his life because he was afraid and felt inadequate. However, God had appointed him as a prophet to nations reminding him that before he was formed, He knew him. Jeremiah's primary message to the people was one of impending judgement and exile for the people of Judah due to their disobedience to God. He urged them to turn from their ways back to God. He faced a lot of opposition and persecution as a result of his message and people rejected him. He was isolated and found himself alone in his convictions. He was called "the weeping prophet" due to the deep sorrow he felt for the people's impending fate.

Jeremiah faced some periods of imprisonment. Despite all these, he remained faithful to God and his calling. He continued to speak the words God had given him, even when it seemed dangerous. Throughout Jeremiah's ministry, God's comfort, assurance and grace were always present. I took courage from Jeremiah's story which illustrated the importance of obedience to one's calling even in the face of adversity and opposition. His unwavering faith in God and commitment to delivering God's message both of judgement and hope is inspirational. His legacy was a reminder that God's purpose for us will always prevail despite the challenging circumstances that we face.

Chapter 2
The Emotional Impact of a Life-Altering Diagnosis: Navigating the Depths of Uncertainty

During my time walking the corridors of nursing school, the theoretical discussions about life-altering illnesses, particularly cancer, were just that – academic exercises that seemed far removed from the realm of personal experience. Little did I anticipate that I would become that statistical anomaly, the one in eight who receive a life-changing diagnosis. The news struck with the force of a hurricane. I couldn't believe it. Never in my wildest dream did I expect to be that one in eight. Everything changed from the moment my eyes saw the report. The mental stress that accompanies such a diagnosis is a weight that few words can capture. It's a silent struggle, an internal battle that plays out daily, sometimes hourly. As I reflect on those early days post-diagnosis, the memories are a tapestry of emotions, a rollercoaster ride through hope, despair, resilience and vulnerability.

In nursing school, the theoretical discussions about cancer were clinical and detached. But when faced with my reality, the realness of this diagnosis gave way to raw, unfiltered emotion. The initial shock, the surreal feeling of being thrust into a reality that was not supposed to be mine, left me grappling with the fundamental question – how do you navigate life when the script takes an unexpected turn? Some days, the journey forward felt like a hesitant step into an uncertain future. On other days, the gravity of the diagnosis pulled me ten steps back, back to that moment when the words hung heavy in the air, an unwelcome prognosis that changed everything. The path forward was unclear and uncertainty became a constant companion. One aspect that stood out starkly in those early days was the profound loneliness that accompanies a life-altering diagnosis. Nobody ever told me how isolating the experience would be. All the knowledge I gained over the years was not enough to prepare me for this time. We learned the clinical aspects of illness, but the curriculums did not in any way cover or address the emotional turmoil that patients grapple with when facing a diagnosis that shakes the foundations of their existence.

When confronted with the question of what to do with these unexpected curveballs, I found myself in a space where conventional answers failed to provide solace. There was no guidebook, no roadmap for the emotional terrain that lay ahead. It became evident that the journey toward healing, both physically and emotionally, would be deeply personal. In the depths of vulnerability, I discovered a reservoir of courage and strength within myself — a resilience that only surfaced when faced with the shadows of uncertainty. In those early moments, it was a solitary journey between me and God. I grappled with faith, questioned the heavens and sought solace in the Divine. There were days when the weight of emotion left me without the energy to open the Bible or utter a prayer. It was then that I unearthed the transformative power of worship. In the melody of hymns and the resonance of spiritual lyrics, I found a sanctuary where my soul could find refuge.

It became apparent that before I could open myself to the support of friends and loved ones, I needed to confront and process all the levels of emotions that I felt within. The path to healing involved confronting my deepest fears – an exploration of the corners of my soul that I had never dared to tread. My initial reaction to the diagnosis was a defence mechanism – an instinctive denial that sought refuge in the incredulity of the situation. Cancer? Me? How? It couldn't be. I had no family history of breast cancer, no significant health issues and a commitment to a lifestyle centred around well-being. The initial reaction was a fortress of denial erected to shield me from the stark reality that life had thrown my way.

Yet, denial, as a coping mechanism, is a fragile fortress that eventually crumbles under the weight of truth. When the walls came crashing down, anger surged forth – an indignant rage that questioned the fairness of life. I had meticulously followed the dictates of faith and strived to lead a virtuous life, and yet, I found myself facing an adversary that seemed indifferent to my righteousness. "Why me?" The question echoed in the recesses of my mind, a plea for an answer that would make sense of the senseless. The anger was not just directed at the disease; it was a visceral protest against the perceived injustice of a fate that seemed incongruent with a life dedicated to faith and goodness. The quest for answers became a relentless pursuit, a craving for a justification that remained elusive. The more I sought explanations, the more emotionally drained I became. It was a cycle of frustration and despair, a journey through the complexities of existential questioning that seemed to have no end.

It was only when I turned the question around, reframing it from "Why me?" to "Why not me?" that a subtle shift occurred. Amid the emotional storm, I began to grasp the transformative power of perspective. It was a paradigm shift that nudged me toward a deeper understanding of the human experience – an acceptance that adversity is a universal companion, an uninvited guest that knocks on every door, regardless of virtue or vice. In those pivotal moments, I clung to the promises embedded in the Holy Scriptures. The journey through the Bible became a source of solace and inspiration. The words of Jeremiah 29:11 resonated with newfound significance – promises of hope and an expected end, a future that transcended the confines of diagnosis.

As I navigated the emotional landscape of uncertainty, certain scriptures became my anchors. The steadfast love of the Divine, the promises of a hopeful future, and the assurance that every adversity carried within it the seeds of transformative growth – all became beacons of light in the caverns of despair.

"'For I know the plans that I have towards you,' declares the Lord, 'Plans to prosper you and not to harm you, plans to give you hope and a future.'" – Jeremiah 29:11

It was a declaration of faith that echoed through the depths of my soul. It was a reminder that the good Lord still had His hand on my life and that nothing takes Him by surprise. The emotional turbulence began to find a rhythm – a rhythm that harmonized with the promises of a good Father. The emotional impact of a life-altering diagnosis, I discovered, is not a linear journey. It's a series of experiences, a kaleidoscope of emotions that range from the depths of despair to the heights of hope. It's a journey through the valleys of vulnerability, where courage is not the absence of fear but the triumph over it.

In the crucible of uncertainty, I found an unexpected reservoir of strength — an inner fortitude that emerged when the foundations of normalcy crumbled. The emotional landscape, once marked by the footprints of denial and anger, gradually transformed into a terrain of acceptance and resilience. The process of emotional healing did not happen as quickly as expected but was a gradual process; an unravelling and understanding of God's love for me, like the petals of a resilient flower that blooms in the harshest of climates. It involved confronting the shadows, navigating the nuances of grief, and embracing the evolving narrative of a life redefined by a diagnosis.

Gratitude, too, was something that emerged out of the turmoil, as a companion on this journey. Gratitude for the moments of respite, the grace that permeated the ability to breathe, the spaces between the storms. It became a practice — a deliberate acknowledgement of the small victories, the glimmers of light that pierced through the darkness; hope that can be seen and felt at the end of the tunnel. As I reflect on the emotional impact of a life-altering diagnosis, I am reminded that the human spirit is remarkably resilient. In the crucible of adversity, we unearth reservoirs of strength that lie dormant until summoned by the call of necessity. It's a journey of self-discovery, a pilgrimage through the recesses of the soul that leads to a profound understanding of the fragility and resilience inherent in the human experience.

The emotional impact, though often shrouded in silence, is a testament to the indomitable spirit that resides within each of us. It's a journey that transcends the boundaries of diagnosis, weaving a narrative of courage, vulnerability and the enduring power of the human heart. In the tapestry of emotions, I found not only the hues of sorrow but also the vibrant colours of hope, resilience and the unyielding spirit that refuses to be defined by the shadows of uncertainty.

I leaned on some scriptural verses that got me through the early stages of dealing with a life-altering diagnosis. The Father's promises for us as His children can be found in His words.

1. Jeremiah 29:11 (New International Version):

   "'For I know the plans I have for you,' declares the Lord, 'Plans for welfare and not for evil, to give you a future.'"

2. John 16:33 (New International Version):

   "I have told you these things, so that in Me you may have peace. In this world, you will have trouble, but take heart, I have overcome the world."

3. Matthew 11:28–30 (New International Version):

   "Come to Me, all you who are weary and burdened, and I will give you rest. Take My yoke upon you and learn from Me, for I am gentle and humble in heart, and you will find rest for your souls. For My yoke is easy and My burden is light."

4. Philippians 4:19 (New International Version):

   "And my God will meet all your needs according to the riches of His glory in Christ Jesus."

5. Isaiah 41:10 (New International Version):

   "So do not fear, for I am with you; do not be dismayed, for I am your God. I will strengthen you and help you; I will uphold you with My righteous right hand."

6. Romans 8:28 (New International Version):

   "And we know that in all things God works for the good of those who love Him, who have been called according to His purpose."

7. Psalm 23:1 (New International Version):

   "The Lord is my shepherd; I shall not want."

8. Isaiah 40:31 (New International Version):

   "But those who hope in the Lord will renew their strength. They will soar on wings like eagles; they will run and not grow weary, they will walk and not be faint."

9. Matthew 6:33 (New International Version):

   "But seek first His kingdom and His righteousness, and all these things will be given to you as well."

10. John 14:27 (New International Version):

    "Peace I leave with you; My peace I give you. I do not give to you as the world gives. Do not let your hearts be troubled and do not be afraid."

11. Proverbs 3:5–6 (New International Version):

    "Trust in the Lord with all your heart and lean not on your understanding; in all your ways submit to Him, and He will make your paths straight."

These verses are just a small selection, and the Bible contains many more promises that provide guidance, assurance and comfort to believers. Taking time to interpret and understand these verses for ourselves gives us the peace we need in trying times. It took a conversation I had with the surgical nurse to make me reflect. She said, "Why are you downcast and acting as if your life is over? You were diagnosed with DCIS which is early stage. You should be happy that it was caught early and thank God for saving your life instead of acting as if the world has come to an end." I went further searching the Scriptures and there right in front of me was the good news, the word of God that remains the same yesterday, today and forever.

1. Isaiah 41:10 (NIV): "So do not fear, for I am with you; do not be dismayed, for I am your God. I will strengthen you and help you; I will uphold you with My righteous right hand."

2. Psalm 34:4 (NIV): "I sought the Lord, and He answered me; He delivered me from all my fears."

3. 2 Timothy 1:7 (NIV): "For the Spirit God gave us does not make us timid, but gives us power, love and self-discipline."

4. Psalm 27:1 (NIV): "The Lord is my light and my salvation – whom shall I fear? The Lord is the stronghold of my life – of whom shall I be afraid?"

5. Deuteronomy 31:6 (NIV): "Be strong and courageous. Do not be afraid or terrified because of them, for the Lord your God goes with you; He will never leave you nor forsake you."

6. Joshua 1:9 (NIV): "Have I not commanded you? Be strong and courageous. Do not be afraid; do not be discouraged, for the Lord your God will be with you wherever you go."

7. 1 John 4:18 (NIV): "There is no fear in love. But perfect love drives out fear because fear has to do with punishment. The one who fears is not made perfect in love."

8. Philippians 4:6–7 (NIV): "Do not be anxious about anything, but in every situation, by prayer and petition, with thanksgiving, present your requests to God. And the peace of God, which transcends all understanding, will guard your hearts and your minds in Christ Jesus."

9. Psalm 56:3–4 (NIV): "When I am afraid, I put my trust in You. In God, whose word I praise – in God I trust and am not afraid. What can mere mortals do to me?"

10. John 14:27 (NIV): "Peace I leave with you; My peace I give you. I do not give to you as the world gives. Do not let your hearts be troubled and do not be afraid."

These passages emphasize the strength, comfort, and peace that can be found in faith and trust in God. They serve as powerful reminders that we can overcome fear through our connection with a Higher Power.

Chapter 3
The Role of Faith in Coping with a Diagnosis

Facing a challenging medical diagnosis, faith plays a crucial role in coping and navigating the complexities of the situation. Faith is a source of hope and comfort during difficult times. Finding hope in God's Word not just in the scripture but also through music, I got into the act of real worship, and on some days I just got lost in the words of some of the worship songs. The words and melodies can be a source of inspiration fostering a sense of peace and tranquillity even in uncertainty. I would play and replay some songs over and over again because it fed my soul and I felt a sense of peace. Some days, words failed me. I couldn't pray, but worship never left my tongue. Worship is a form of expression, and it becomes a powerful means of expression when words fail.

If we believe that God's promise for us is good and not evil, then we have to accept God's will for us. Faith is built on the unconventional circumstance that "just because there is evidence of an enemy, it doesn't mean God is absent." I remember hearing this being preached by Apostle Greg during a conference in church and it hit me and spoke directly to my soul. I had to remind myself of this fact, seeing the hand of God in how my diagnosis came about. God's plan is ultimately for the good of His followers. This perspective can help us accept the reality of a diagnosis and to find purpose amid suffering.

Clinging to Faith in Healing

After the biopsy I prayed, my husband prayed, my family prayed and I believed God for total healing that what was found earlier would not be seen after the biopsy. I hoped and prayed that it would be gone, that it would disappear from wherever it came from. To be told that it was malignant, I had so many questions running through my mind. Did that take away the healing? I believe my healing took place from the start. The circumstances surrounding my diagnosis were already proof that God's hand was in it. Seeking medical treatment did not in any way alter my faith and belief in God. I believe medical professionals are God's gift to us and instruments used in bringing forth healing. Coping with a medical diagnosis is a multifaceted process. Many Christians find a balance between their spiritual beliefs and practical strategies for emotional and physical well-being. So through the turmoil and questions, it all came down to one point, that nothing takes God by surprise and that His presence has never left me.

Shaken by Trials but not Stirred

Only a few people knew what I was going through at the time. "Thank God, I don't look like what I have been through was my story." I believe it was all down to God's grace. Apart from my initial reaction, I felt a sense of calm. I would normally panic over things but it was different this time. I felt that I had no other choice but to drop this heavy burden at the altar. I had cried out all the tears and ran out of tears, so the only option available was to take it to the One who knew the end from the beginning. Some actions or words would make me cry but as soon as I dealt with those emotions, I would be OK afterwards. My resilience in the face of adversity and ability to maintain a steady and composed demeanour despite being tested by life's trials was only by His grace. Enduring hardships without allowing them to fundamentally change my character, values or resolve, is just down to my faith and belief, that all things work together for our good.

Where is God in All of This?

Facing my diagnosis in the early stages I asked myself this question and I am sure that most people and my family did as well, the truth is that God has never left. Before He formed me, He knew me. Nothing takes Him by surprise. He knows the end from the beginning and all the in-between. The Creator of the universe. Rather than ask myself this question, I chose gratitude. It could have been a different story but for grace.

The power of gratitude and positivity during setbacks is profound and can significantly impact one's well-being and resilience. It shifts our perspective instead of focusing solely on what went wrong, and it encourages us to acknowledge and focus on what is still positive and good in our lives. So I shifted my focus from worry and fear to thanksgiving. I tried to focus on the present. I was still alive, my family was doing great and I had a lot to be thankful for.

Having a positive mindset can enhance resilience and the ability to bounce back from adversity when facing setbacks. It can help navigate challenges more effectively and recover more quickly. Gratitude has been linked to a reduction in stress levels. It helps keep the focus on what you are thankful for, even in difficult times. It can trigger the release of stress-reducing hormones and promote a sense of calm. Expressing gratitude and maintaining a positive mindset are associated with improved emotional well-being. Eventually opening up to friends when I was ready to share, gave me that extra covering I felt supported by friends and families, and it became even more crucial in my healing journey and fostered a positive environment. Having a growth mindset is the belief that challenges and setbacks are opportunities for growth and learning. Gratitude and positivity are aligned with a growth mindset, encouraging one to view setbacks as a chance to develop resilience and acquire skills. Incorporating gratitude practices such as keeping a journal or expressing thanks regularly and cultivating a positive mindset can be transformative, especially during setbacks. It can also have a positive effect on physical health and overall life satisfaction.

Reflecting on the early days after my diagnosis, it felt as if I was sinking into a very big hole. I was so scared of the prognosis and because my focus was on everything that was about to go wrong, I saw no way out of it. As for human beings: fear is an evolutionary response that plays a crucial role in our survival; it triggers the fight or flight response. Fear can evoke various psychological responses including anxiety, stress and heightened awareness. In several places in the Bible, we are instructed not to fear, rather we should trust in God's promises and that indeed He is with us; that He will never leave us or forsake us. Isaiah 41:10 says, "Do not fear for I am with you; do not be dismayed for I am your God. I will strengthen you and help you, I will uphold you with My righteous hand."

The Bible tells us that perfect love casts out fear. 1 John 4:18 emphasises the relationship between love and fear. There is no fear in love, and the one who fears is not made perfect in love. Having a deep understanding and experience of God's love can diminish unhealthy fears.

As the days went by, I was encouraged by Philippians 4:6-7,

"Do not be anxious about anything, but in every situation by prayer and petition make your requests known to God."

It encourages us to bring our anxieties to God in prayer. God is calling us to overcome unhealthy fear through faith, trust and understanding of God's love and promises. Facing and overcoming fear can be an integral part of personal growth and development. Confronting fears, whether they are related to personal challenges, relationships or self-discovery, can lead to increased resilience and a broader sense of empowerment.

The time it takes to digest bad news varies from person to person. Personally, it took me weeks to accept my diagnosis. I had to go through a cycle of reactions. The initial reaction included shock, sadness, anger and a sense of disbelief. However, the presence of a strong support system helped contribute to a faster acceptance and understanding of my diagnosis. Having friends, family or professional support can provide comfort and assistance in processing different information. Emotions may fluctuate from time to time and it is important to note that each individual has a unique way of coping and that there isn't a significant time frame.

Here I was facing yet another curve ball. It wasn't too long ago that I had dealt with a health scare, and the first thing I did apart from crying was to pray. Prayer is fundamental when faced with challenges. Philippians 4:6-7 encourages us to present our request to God through prayer, with the promise that God's peace will guide our hearts and minds. Another thing I did was to depend on God's Word. He did not bring me this far in my life to leave me. Reflecting on the passages from the Bible was important for my mental health. Psalms 23 embodied all I felt at that time. Some days I had to dig deep and remind myself of God's promise for my life. We must key into our faith during difficult times because the Word of God has given us all that we need to get through those moments. Philippians 4:13 says that I can do all things through Christ who strengthens me.

Practicing Self-Compassion in the Face of Adversity

Self-compassion serves as a vital tool in navigating life's setbacks; offering a framework of kindness, understanding and acceptance during times of difficulty. It is a cornerstone of emotional resilience that fosters strength and fortitude in the face of adversity. In my journey, I've learned the importance of extending compassion to oneself, particularly when facing unexpected challenges. Rather than succumbing to harsh self-criticism or blaming myself for circumstances beyond my control, I've embraced a more nurturing and supportive approach to my feelings.

Even when confronted with setbacks, such as my unexpected diagnosis, I resisted the temptation to berate myself or dwell on perceived shortcomings. Instead, I acknowledged the complexity of my situation and offered myself the same level of compassion and understanding that I would readily extend to a dear friend. This shift in mindset has been transformative, empowering me to confront difficulties with resilience and grace. By reframing negative self-talk and embracing a more positive outlook, I've cultivated a sense of emotional well-being that has proven invaluable in navigating life's challenges.

Research supports the notion that practising self-compassion can significantly enhance psychological well-being, leading to lower levels of anxiety and depression. By fostering mindfulness and cultivating a present-moment awareness, self-compassion enables us to focus on constructive actions and solutions, rather than dwelling on past mistakes or future uncertainties. Furthermore, self-compassion bolsters self-efficacy – the belief in one's ability to overcome obstacles – essential for resilience. By treating ourselves with the same kindness and understanding that we would offer to a friend in need, we cultivate a supportive and constructive mindset that fosters growth and adaptation in the face of adversity.

In essence, practising self-compassion is not only an act of kindness towards oneself but also a powerful tool for building resilience and navigating life's challenges with courage and grace. By embracing self-compassion, we empower ourselves to face setbacks with resilience, strength, and unwavering belief in our ability to overcome.

1. Cultivating self-compassion involves acknowledging and validating our emotions, allowing us to process and navigate difficult situations with greater ease.

2. Self-compassion encourages us to recognize our common humanity, understanding that setbacks and challenges are a natural part of the human experience rather than personal failings.

3. By fostering self-compassion, we develop a greater sense of self-worth and acceptance, reducing feelings of shame or inadequacy that may arise during difficult times.

4. Practicing self-compassion can improve our relationships with others, as we become more empathetic and understanding towards their struggles and challenges.

5. Incorporating self-compassion into our daily lives requires practice and mindfulness, but the benefits – including increased resilience, emotional well-being, and overall life satisfaction – are well worth the effort.

Create a Quiet Space

Establish a physical or mental space where you can retreat when things get overwhelming. It could be a quiet room, a corner with comfortable pillows or a mental space you visualise. This creates a sanctuary for moments of calm reflection. I chose walking. I walked seven days a week, and I would walk to the point that I zoomed out. People often confronted me saying they would scream out my name driving past but I wouldn't respond. Walking was my escape route. It was where I would cry, where I found the strength and courage to keep going. Connecting with nature also had a calming effect on my mind and body.

Journaling helped a great deal. I did this to an extent rather than write. I recorded what I was feeling. Doing this can be a cathedralic experience and a way to honour and validate one's feelings. It also provides an opportunity for self-reflection and insight.

Seeking support was something that I did not feel comfortable doing in the early days because I felt that I did not want anyone else bearing my burden and that they wouldn't have the right answers that I was seeking. I also set some boundaries for myself. I said no to certain responsibilities and commitments and most time I just wanted to be by myself. This helped protect my emotional well-being. Solomon would sometimes plead with me to let him into my thoughts. I would only say a few words during the early days. However, honouring your emotions doesn't mean suppressing or ignoring them. It is about acknowledging and allowing yourself to feel, while also taking steps to care for your well-being. Finding moments of serenity is a personal journey and different strategies may work for different people. It is important to experiment with various approaches to discover what resonates best with you during difficult times.

EMPOWERING THE ONE IN EIGHT

Chapter 4
The Necessity of Trials in the Journey of a Believer

Introduction

Facing trials and challenges can contribute to the spiritual growth and maturity of a believer. It provides opportunities for individuals to develop virtues such as patience, perseverance and faith. Trials are often seen as a test of faith. Overcoming trials can strengthen our faith as believers to depend more on God, and through this, our relationship with God is deepened. Challenges are opportunities that aid our character development. Through adversity, we are refined. Just as the refining of precious metal is used figuratively in the Bible to illustrate the kind of trials that we as God's children are called upon to go through. The way to experience the fire of God as refining and not consuming is to trust His promise to bring us through the fire to endless joy.

When believers are faced with afflictions, it is always for refinement; never for destruction. 1 Peter 1:6–7 says, "Now for a little while you may have to suffer various trials, so that the genuineness of your faith, more precious than gold, which though perishable is tested by fire, may resound in praise and glory and honour at the revelation of Jesus Christ."

"Count it all joy, my brethren, when you meet various trials; for you know that the testing of your faith produces steadfastness, and let the steadfastness have its full effect, that you may be perfect and completely lacking in nothing." – James 1:2–4

So in times of setbacks, we need to stay encouraged and trust that even in difficult times, there is a purpose and a greater plan that they might not fully comprehend. This outlook can bring a sense of purpose and acceptance during challenging times.

Why are trials part of lived experiences? I had to search the scriptures for examples of people who faced trying times. I remember studying about Joseph as a child. I remember in Sunday school classes everybody wanted to be Joseph in their family. His brothers sold him into slavery. Genesis 37 tells us the story – he went through a difficult season as a result of that. Through it all, he declared in Genesis 50:20, "As for you, you meant evil against me, but God meant it for good to bring about this present result, to keep my people alive."

Despite all that was happening to Joseph, he chose to fix his gaze on God and chose to rely on Him. Romans 8:28 says, "God causes everything to work together for the good of those who love Him."

Another story that I looked at was that of Shadrach, Meshach and Abednego. Daniel 3 tells us the story of these three men who were thrown into a fiery furnace by King Nebuchadnezzar for refusing to worship a false god. But their faith and devotion to God kept them alive. They were tied up and thrown into a furnace of fire. Daniel 3:24–25 says that King Nebuchadnezzar jumped to his feet, and he was very surprised and asked his advisors, "We tied only three men, and we threw only three men into the fire, look I see four men walking around in the fire, they are not tied up and they are not burned. The fourth man looks like an angel" (Daniel 3:28–29). Nebuchadnezzar responded and said, "Blessed be the God of Shadrach, Meshach and Abednego who has sent His angel and rescued His servants who put their trust in Him, violating the king's command and surrendered their bodies rather than serve or worship any god except their own God. Therefore, I make a decree that any people, nation or population of any language that speaks anything offensive against the God of Shadrach, Meshach and Abednego shall be torn limb from limb and their houses made a rubbish heap because there is no other god who can save in this way." The Bible has so many other examples of people who went through trials and tribulations. Each person who went through a period of hardship grew closer in their relationship with God.

The Purpose of Trials in Spiritual Growth

Trials are not arbitrary obstacles; they are purposeful elements woven into the fabric of a believer's existence. The scriptures, revered as guideposts for spiritual life, consistently emphasise the transformative power embedded in trials. James 1:2–4 encourages believers to "consider it pure joy ... whenever you face trials of many kinds because you know that the testing of your faith produces perseverance. Let perseverance finish its work so that you may be mature and complete, not lacking anything." Here, trials are portrayed as catalysts for the refinement and maturation of one's faith. Trials, when embraced with the right perspective, become a furnace where the impurities of faith are melted away, leaving behind a purified and strengthened belief. This refining process is not meant to break believers but to forge them into resilient vessels capable of weathering life's storms with unwavering trust.

Trials as a Path to Deeper Understanding

While trials are often perceived as challenges to be overcome, they also serve as a gateway to a deeper understanding of God and our devotion to Him. In moments of trial, believers are compelled to seek solace, guidance and strength from a Source beyond themselves. This seeking becomes a transformative journey, leading to a profound connection with the Divine that transcends the superficialities of faith.

The scriptures affirm this transformative potential. Psalm 34:17–18 asserts, "The righteous cry out, and the Lord hears them; He delivers them from all their troubles. The Lord is close to the broken-hearted and saves those who are crushed in spirit." Here, trials are portrayed as an invitation to draw near to the Divine Presence, fostering an intimacy that goes beyond mere intellectual or ritualistic expressions of faith.

Trials as Tests of Faith

Trials, in their essence, serve as tests of faith. In the biblical narrative, numerous figures faced trials that tested the depth and authenticity of their trust in God. Abraham's willingness to sacrifice his son, Job's endurance through immense suffering, and the Israelites' journey through the wilderness – all these stories depict trials as transformative tests that sifted the superficial from the genuine.

In the crucible of trials, believers are presented with an opportunity to examine the foundations of their faith. The Apostle Paul, in 1 Corinthians 3:12–15, employs the metaphor of a builder constructing on different foundations. He asserts that some will build with enduring materials, while others with materials that will not withstand the test of fire. The trials, in this analogy, act as the refining fire that reveals the true nature of the structures built upon faith.

Trials as a Catalyst for Empathy and Compassion

Beyond personal growth, trials equip believers with a unique capacity for empathy and compassion. Having faced challenges, believers are better positioned to understand and support others in their journeys through difficulties. The empathy born out of shared struggles fosters a sense of communal strength and unity among believers, echoing the biblical principle of bearing one another's burdens (Galatians 6:2).

Jesus Himself, in His earthly life, exemplified the intertwining of trials, empathy and compassion. The Gospel narratives portray Him as not just a Divine figure but as compassionate, and One who endured trials, allowing Him to empathise with the human condition. Hebrews 4:15 captures this empathetic nature, stating that Jesus "was tempted in every way, just as we are – yet He did not sin." Here, trials become a bridge connecting believers to the compassion of a Higher

Power who intimately understands the challenges of human existence.

Trials as Catalysts for Personal Transformation

Trials are there to challenge us as believers to face our fears and weaknesses. At the same time, they refine our character and spiritual maturity, and strengthen our faith in God's Word. The Apostle Peter, in 1 Peter 1:6–7, articulates this transformative process, stating that believers "may have had to suffer grief in all kinds of trials. These have come so that the proven genuineness of your faith – of greater worth than gold, which perishes even though refined by fire – may result in praise, glory, and honour when Jesus Christ is revealed."

In this perspective, trials are not arbitrary hardships but intentional instruments for shaping believers into vessels capable of radiating the authenticity and strength of their faith. The analogy of refining gold through fire underscores the notion that trials are not meant to diminish believers but to reveal the genuine and enduring nature of their faith. Going through my journey, I started to look at my setbacks as a period of refining, just as gold has to go through the fire to become what it is, therefore trials are not meant to discourage us as believers but to reveal the genuine and enduring nature of our faith.

The Role of Faith in Navigating Trials

Faith, as a guiding force, plays a pivotal role in how believers navigate trials. It provides a framework for interpreting challenges, a source of strength in moments of weakness, and a foundation for hope when faced with adversity. Hebrews 11, often referred to as the "faith hall of fame," recounts the stories of individuals who, through faith, "conquered kingdoms, administered justice and gained what was promised" (Hebrews 11:33).

The narrative of faith in Hebrews 11 emphasises that, despite trials and uncertainties, faith becomes the anchor that steadies believers in the storm. It is the assurance of things hoped for and the conviction of things not seen (Hebrews 11:1). In the face of trials, faith becomes the lens through which believers perceive the unseen Hand guiding them, the unseen promises sustaining them, and the unseen future awaiting them.

In the journey of a believer, trials are not mere obstacles to be endured; they are transformative milestones on the path to spiritual maturity. They refine, deepen, and strengthen the fabric of faith, shaping individuals into resilient, empathetic and compassionate beings. While trials may be uncomfortable, even painful, they serve a purpose beyond the immediate challenges they present.

James 1:12 encapsulates the essence of trials in the life of a believer, "Blessed is the one who perseveres under trial because, having stood the test, that person will receive the crown of life that the Lord has promised to those who love Him." The endurance through trials, fuelled by love and anchored in faith, becomes a testament to the resilience and enduring nature of a believer's connection with the Divine. In the grand tapestry of faith, trials emerge not as disruptions but as integral threads, weaving a story of growth, transformation and unwavering trust in the providence of a loving Creator.

Chapter 5
The Significance of Friendship During Difficult Times: A Personal Journey

Friendship has always held a special place in my life. I've often believed in the power of a few solid connections rather than a multitude of acquaintances. This conviction was put to the test when I relocated to Saudi Arabia, bringing with me the challenge of forging new friendships in a foreign land and leaving behind solid friendships which have been built over the years – some of which still stand and some of which fizzled out due to distance and it being one-sided. Juggling the responsibilities of raising three children under the age of three, I found myself immersed in a whirlwind of domestic duties and had limited opportunities to socialise. A year later I was back working full-time in the hospital so there wasn't enough time to get acquainted with a lot of people. However, I was happy with the few friends that I had made.

My initial encounters in the expatriate community echoed the reminiscent struggles of secondary school, where cliques seemed to dominate social dynamics. As a free spirit, I preferred forging connections on my terms, based on genuine alignment of spirits rather than conforming to predefined groups. The transient nature of expatriate life meant encountering people from diverse backgrounds, enriching my experiences but making it a prolonged process to find kindred spirits. People generally did not want you laying claims on their friends, as they had known them the longest or had built some kind of friendship with them. So it was a feeling of being stuck as acquaintances. I felt if I was going to invite someone out for lunch I had to invite her friend as well. It took a lot of adjustment to settle in an expatriate community.

It took several months before I felt a genuine connection with a few individuals, and even longer to open up about the challenges that life had thrown my way. Despite having numerous acquaintances, I held back from sharing my medical diagnosis with many. Historically, I had been the pillar of strength for others, a source of guidance and assistance – always the positive one and forever ready to affirm. However, finding myself on the receiving end of support was uncharted territory for me, and vulnerability was a facet of my personality that I rarely revealed. I struggled with the option of sharing my diagnosis. I knew there was no way I could keep it to myself; it was such a huge burden to bear alone. Yes, I had told my family but we were all scattered all over the world, and I needed a support network that was present.

Suddenly the thread of friendship once decorative became a vital lifeline as I grappled with the weight of uncertainty and vulnerability. I chose to confide in those I held dear. Little did I know that this decision would unravel a tapestry of emotions, unveiling both the resilience and fragility of these connections.

The first person I confided in was someone who I looked up to as a big sister. She was always positive in her thinking and a woman of great faith whom I admired – a mentor of sorts. Her calm and composed reaction contrasted with my emotional turmoil. Instead of sympathy towards one of my early questions — which was, "Why me?" — she offered a perspective that startled me, "Why not you?" This question, accompanied by a reassuring prayer, initiated a journey of introspection. While her words provided spiritual comfort, I realised I craved a different form of support — a friend with whom I could share the raw emotions and vulnerability that come with a life-altering diagnosis. Back on reflection, I realised that her words strengthened my faith at that time. There was no room for self-pity; it was the firm support that I needed to keep going.

The second person I chose to confide in was a close friend who was also dealing with health issues of her own. As I shared my biopsy results, I saw the shock on her face, and though she attempted to console me, I felt that she already had a lot going on and I felt guilty putting my burden on her. The disparity in our experiences made me acutely aware of the unique challenges that accompany sharing difficult news. One commonality emerged from these early experiences — people, even well-meaning friends, often struggled to respond appropriately to the mention of illness. Recognising that cancer was an uncomfortable topic, I decided to limit sharing my diagnosis to a select few, particularly as I prepared for an upcoming operation.

The response from my closest friend, however, left me feeling isolated. The initial prayers were followed by an unexpected silence, and the lack of subsequent communication became a source of inner turmoil. As I walked daily, tears streamed down my face. I questioned why the support I expected wasn't materialising. In my attempt to understand, I withdrew, seeking solace in God.

It was during this introspective period that I heard a reassuring message: "I am what you seek. In Me, you will find peace."

This revelation prompted a shift in my perspective on friendship and support. I acknowledged that my friends, though dear, had not navigated such situations before and might not comprehend how to respond. I reconciled with the fact that they couldn't provide what I sought. It was a pivotal moment of accepting that my peace would come from within and from a higher Source. As I made peace with my emotions, I encountered friends who genuinely wanted to support me but grappled with their uncertainty. One friend, expressing concern about being overbearing, inadvertently highlighted the disparity between my perceived needs and their understanding of what support should entail. In this moment, I realised the importance of articulating one's needs, especially in times of vulnerability.

While physical presence holds immense value during challenging times, I learned that friendship, like any relationship, evolves, and people respond to crises in diverse ways. My journey through this period of difficulty allowed me to redefine my expectations, appreciate the diverse ways people express care, and find solace in my resilience.

The significance of friendship during difficult times extends beyond conventional expectations, delving into the complexities of individual responses and evolving dynamics. My journey unveiled the importance of open communication, understanding varying expressions of support, and ultimately finding internal peace. In navigating life-altering medical issues, the tapestry of friendship proved resilient, woven with threads of empathy, resilience, and the recognition that each friend contributes to the fabric of support in their own unique way. As I continue on this journey, I embrace the evolving nature of friendship and the profound impact it has on navigating life's challenges.

I often reflected on biblical examples of great friendships that are highlighted for their loyalty, support and love. The book of Job tells us that when Job faced persecution (Job 2:11–13), his friends Eliphaz, Bildad and Zophar, initially provided a good example of good friendship by sitting with him in silence during his time of suffering. However, their attempts to explain Job's suffering later lead to conflict. Despite this, the initial act of silence and companionship reflects a form of solidarity.

So no matter what a friend is going through, showing up and being there for a friend goes a long way to help. The Bible also showcases the relationship between Jesus and His disciples – especially Peter, James and John. It demonstrates the essence of friendship. Jesus shared His teachings and experiences and ultimately sacrificed Himself for the sake of His friends. The Last Supper is a poignant example of Jesus emphasising the importance of love and service among His followers.

Some of these great friendships in the Bible are characterised by various qualities that reflect deep bonds, loyalty and mutual support. True friendship in the Bible is marked by unwavering loyalty: friends stand by each other through thick and thin, even in the face of adversity. The loyalty of friends like Jonathan to David and Ruth to Naomi is evident in their commitment and sacrifices for each other.

Biblical friendship often involves selfless acts and sacrificial love. Jesus as the ultimate example laid down His life for his friends (John 15:13). The willingness to put the needs and well-being of the friend above one's own is a recurring theme in strong biblical friendships. Great friendships are evident in times of trouble, friends provide comfort, encouragement and support during challenging moments.

Effective communication and openness are crucial in biblical friendship. Friends share their thoughts, feelings and concerns. Paul's letter to his friends and disciples, like Timothy, demonstrates the importance of staying connected and providing guidance through communication.

Forgiveness is a recurring theme in the Bible. Great friendships often involve a willingness to forgive. Peter's denial of Jesus and subsequent reconciliation exemplify that forgiveness and reconciliation are characteristics that can deepen friendship (John 21:15-19).

Shared experiences contribute to the depths of biblical friendships. Jesus and His disciples shared various life experiences and these shared moments created a sense of comradeship and strengthened the bond between friends.

Dealing with disappointments in friendship can be challenging, but it's an inevitable part of human relationships. Reflecting on how I felt at first, I realised that my expectations were not realistic and that the disappointment I felt was a result of misunderstanding. Thankfully I was able to communicate openly about my feelings. Managing expectations or having realistic expectations is important. It's important to understand that people may make mistakes and adjust expectations to help prevent future disappointments.

Some tips on supporting a friend who has been diagnosed with a life-altering medical issue are crucial and your presence and understanding can make a significant difference. Here are some ways you can offer support

Express empathy – Expressing empathy and understanding, lets your friend know you are there for them, and that you care about their wellbeing. It could be in affirmative words, acts of kindness (like making time to take them out), cooking a healthy meal and finding time to speak to them regularly.

Active Listening – Be a good listener, and allow your friend to share their feelings, thoughts and concerns without judgement. Sometimes people simply need someone to talk to and share their emotions with.

Educate yourself – Learn about the medical condition your friend is facing and understand the challenges and treatment options. This can help you provide more informed and empathetic support.

Offer practical help – Ask your friend if there are specific ways you can assist them practically. This could include helping with daily tasks, providing transportation to medical appointments or meal preps.

Respect their wishes – Respect your friend's autonomy and decision. Everyone copes with illness differently and your friend may have specific preferences about how they want to handle their medical situation.

Check in regularly – Regularly check in on your friend, even if it is just a brief message to let them know you're thinking of them. Consistent communication shows your ongoing support.

Be flexible and adaptable – Your friend's needs and emotions may change over time and your support should be flexible enough to accommodate those changes.

Accompany them to appointments – Especially if they feel anxious or overwhelmed, having a supportive presence can provide comfort during challenging times.

Respect their privacy – Whilst it is important to offer support, some individuals may prefer to keep a certain aspect of their medical journey private. Always ask before sharing information with others.

Celebrate – Celebrate positive moments and small victories in your friend's journey, whether it is a good medical report or a day when they feel well.

Be patient – You must recognise that your friend may go through a range of emotions including fear, frustration, and sadness. Be patient and understanding, allowing them space to process their feelings.

Encourage self-care – Offer to take them to activities that bring them joy and relaxation and offer to participate in these activities with them.

Provide emotional support – Let your friend know it is OK to express their emotions. Sometimes just having someone to share the emotional burden with can be incredibly comforting.

Friendship plays a significant role during difficult times for several reasons offering emotional, psychological and practical support. In essence, it serves as a pillar of strength, providing emotional, psychological and practical support. The bonds formed during adversity can deepen, creating lasting connections that contribute to personal growth and resilience.

Chapter 6
Setbacks and Triumphs

I remember my university days spent trying to find myself. Most of the time I felt lost trying to find myself. I finished university and started working. Going on dates wasn't a problem – I was inundated with guys. However, some of them did not meet the criteria of what I was looking for. Money was not an issue. I was comfortable. I was a born hustler and right from an early age, my parents had raised me to be able to fend for myself. I just wanted a God-fearing man who was hardworking and supportive and whom I could build a future with.

On this particular day, whilst in my room, I cried out to God. I wailed because I was tired of meeting the wrong people. I remember in that moment of sadness asking God to have His way in my life and asking that the next person I meet is the one that ticks all the right boxes and that I also tick his boxes. That night I poured my heart out to God in prayer and afterwards had a deep sense of relief and felt in my spirit that God had heard. A couple of weeks later I was online on a webpage called "HI5" and I remember browsing through one of the groups that I belonged to. I saw the name SOLOJI and I thought, "How strange! How is that somebody's real name?" I plucked up the courage and I sent a message, asking if that was his real name. A few hours later he replied saying that it was a combination of his first and last name. We carried on chatting for a few minutes online. I remember logging off and getting a message a few hours later with him asking me for my number. There was no way I wanted to give him my number – he could be anyone. How was I sure he was who he said he was? But he was persistent. So, I thought, why not make him work hard for it? I created a code mixed with digits from my mobile number and asked him to solve it and that if he got it right that would be my number. Up until this day, I didn't know what made me do it, so I went to sleep only to wake up the next day with missed calls on my phone. So I did not call back because I did not recognise the number, and never in my wildest dream did I expect that it would be him. A few hours later my phone rang and the deep voice at the end of the phone said, "Hello. Is this Ify?" I said yes and he responded saying, "This is 'Soloji.'" I nearly passed out. How? I couldn't believe that he solved the code. It turned out he had called several numbers and still was patient enough before getting it right. At that moment I knew there was something special about him. We got to know each other and the rest – as they say – is history. Fourteen years later we are still doing life together. He ticked all the right boxes, and then some, and indeed I couldn't have asked for a better husband. God is faithful to His word. My friends and family would always tease me, saying they don't know what my life would have been like without King Sol in it. My faith is so important to me and finding someone who shares similar values was important to me too.

You see, I have always known God. I grew up in a God-fearing household, and morning and night devotion was never missed in our house. At the break of dawn we would automatically find ourselves with my brothers walking towards the living room as if we were in a trance moving to the sound of singing echoing from either my mum or dad. We went to church every Wednesday and

Sunday and volunteered in different Christian activities. My dad was a member of many Christian organisations, one of which is the Gideon International Bible Society. Our weekends, Saturdays to be precise, were spent stamping boxes of Bibles with the Bible Society address. So, whenever I come across one of the Gideon Bibles in the hotel room, I smile and get an overwhelming sense of pride, and I also flip the pages to see what country the Bible was sponsored from.

I vividly recall the day of our return journey from Nigeria after a joyous traditional wedding celebration. Little did we know, our journey would take an unexpected turn into the heart of danger. On the morning of 20 April 2009, the second day after our traditional wedding, we embarked on our trip back to Lagos. Despite the hustle and bustle of preparations, my husband's message of protection and love lingered in my mind. Little did I know, those words would become a lifeline in the hours to come.

As we set off in our brand-new Toyota Camry, adorned with the blessings of our family, little did we anticipate the imminent threat lurking ahead. Amid our journey, a simple oversight led us back to our village to retrieve forgotten keys – a detour that would alter the course of our day. As we approached a deserted junction between Nnewi and Oba, the tranquillity of the surroundings was shattered by the deafening sound of gunshots. Panic and fear gripped us as we realized the gravity of the situation. With nowhere to hide, we found ourselves at the mercy of armed robbers wreaking havoc. In those moments of terror, each member of my family responded differently. Our driver, typically a tower of strength, was visibly shaken. My brother remained remarkably calm, a testament to his unwavering faith. My mother, usually anxious, found solace in silent prayers, her trust unwavering. And my father, a man of steadfast faith, led us in prayer, his unwavering belief a source of comfort.

Amidst the chaos, I found myself grappling with fear and uncertainty. Yet, as I called out to my husband for prayers, a newfound sense of faith and courage enveloped me. In the face of danger, we clung to each other, united in prayer and resilience. Miraculously, we emerged unscathed from the ordeal, our lives spared by Divine intervention. Though the memory of that fateful day lingers, it serves as a poignant reminder of the fragility of life and the power of faith.

As we drove away from the harrowing scene, the weight of what we had just experienced began to sink in. Our hearts were heavy with gratitude for our miraculous escape yet burdened by the realisation of the lives lost and the violence that had unfolded before our eyes. Arriving home safely felt like a dream, a surreal moment of relief amidst the lingering echoes of gunshots and the stark reality of what could have been. But even as we sought solace within the familiar walls of our home, the memory of that day haunted us – a constant reminder of life's fragility.

In the days that followed, we grappled with the aftermath of our ordeal, each of us processing the trauma in our own way. For me, the fear and anxiety lingered long after the danger had passed, manifesting in sleepless nights and restless days filled with apprehension. But amidst the darkness, there were moments of light – moments of grace and resilience that reaffirmed our faith in the goodness of humanity and the power of love. We were overwhelmed by the outpouring of support from friends, family, and even strangers, whose prayers and words of encouragement lifted our spirits and helped us heal.

As we reflected on our journey, we were filled with a renewed sense of purpose and gratitude for the gift of life. We resolved to live each day with intention, cherishing every moment and embracing the blessings that surrounded us. In the months that followed, we found strength in each other, drawing closer as a family and leaning on our faith to guide us through the challenges that lay ahead. Together, we navigated the ups and downs of life, finding solace in the knowledge that we were never alone.

Looking back on that fateful day, I am reminded of the resilience of the human spirit and the power of faith to overcome even the darkest of times. Though the scars of our ordeal may never fully fade, they serve as a testament to our strength and resilience in the face of adversity. And as we continue our journey forward, we do so with hearts full of gratitude and a deep sense of appreciation for the precious gift of life. For in the end, it is our faith, our love, and our unwavering belief in the goodness of humanity that will see us through even the darkest of nights.

This experience taught me so many lessons – to not take the Word of God for granted. Since that day, my life has never been the same. I live my life as one with purpose, and I have recognized my relevance here on earth. Once you know you are a vital part of the gospel nothing can uproot you. The anointing is surely perfecting all that concerns me. The circumstances around me could not steal my confession, I ended up drowning all the noise around me with the word of God.

Faith

During our white wedding, I had requested gift vouchers from Mother Care because that was how keen I was to start a family – as soon as I said, "I do." However, it took a year and a few months of trying to conceive. After my son turned one, I knew that I wouldn't wait long to try for another baby. I remember my aunty praying over my son on his birthday and declaring that by the time next year, I would have twins. I remember feeling shocked and laughing, "What? From where?" I had no history of twins in my family or Solomon's family; plus, I was already struggling to look after one, not even to mention two! So, it took further explanation from her and the reassurance that God always provides. After that, I agreed and said "amen" to the prayer.

A few months later, I was feeling nauseous and had missed a period. I did a pregnancy test which came back positive, I went to the hospital for a scan and behold there were two sacs and two hearts. One more shocking detail was that there was a two-week difference between both sacs which meant that I had conceived them separately two weeks apart. I couldn't believe it. I immediately called Solomon and we both screamed out in shock of course. The next person I told was my aunty who had prophesied. The rest is history. So you see, my life has always been full of God's goodness and mercies – He has always come through for me and my family.

During the pregnancy, not only was it high risk with frequent scans but also I had done a cervical smear test which came back "abnormal" the week I had found out that I was pregnant. Of course, it was nine months of worry, feeling anxious and praying that God's promise would prevail. Six weeks after I had the twins, I went back and did a biopsy and the results came back negative. It has been negative since then. The Bible says that those who know their God will be strong and do exploits. A life free of trials and tribulations has never been the promise, but rather the promise is that God will be with us through the storms of life.

In the face of life-altering setbacks, discovering a purpose-driven life becomes a beacon of hope and resilience. It is during these challenging times that the profound truth echoed in the Bible, resonates deeply: "Before we were formed, He knew us." This sentiment becomes a guiding light, a reminder that our existence is not arbitrary but intricately woven into the fabric of a greater design.

As we navigate the complexities of our existence, setbacks can catalyse self-reflection. They prompt us to explore the deeper meaning of our journey and question the purpose behind our unique challenges. It's in these moments that we often unearth a reservoir of strength we never knew we possessed, and a newfound determination to live authentically and with purpose.

The process of embracing a purpose-driven life after facing setbacks is akin to cultivating a garden after a storm. The adversity may have swept through, leaving destruction in its wake, but within the fertile soil of our experiences lies the potential for growth, resilience, and the blossoming of a purposeful existence.

In searching for our purpose, it's essential to recognise the multifaceted nature of our being. Beyond the roles we play in our daily lives, there exists a deeper essence – a unique blend of talents, passions and values that define us. It is by aligning with these core aspects of ourselves that we begin to unravel the tapestry of our purpose.

Moreover, a purpose-driven life often extends beyond personal fulfilment; it encompasses the positive impact we can have on others and the world around us. Acts of kindness, compassion and service become integral components of our purpose; transforming setbacks into opportunities for empathy and connection.

As we embark on this journey of purpose, it's crucial to approach it with a sense of openness and adaptability. Life's setbacks can alter our course, but they need not dictate our destination. Embracing a purpose-driven life involves being attuned to the evolving nature of our aspirations and the ever-changing landscape of our personal and collective experiences.

In essence, setbacks can be viewed as a recalibration of our life's compass, guiding us toward a truer north – our purpose. Through introspection, resilience and a commitment to live authentically, we not only navigate the challenges that come our way but also transform them into stepping stones toward a more meaningful and purposeful existence.

As you embark on the path of self-discovery, consider the things that make your heart beat a little faster and your spirit come alive. What activities bring you joy; not just in fleeting moments, but in a sustained and profound way? It's within these moments of joy where clues to your purpose often reside. Whether it's a creative pursuit, a cause that ignites your passion, or a skill that you effortlessly excel in, these are the threads that, when woven together, form the fabric of your purpose.

Ultimately, the pursuit of purpose is a lifelong endeavour; a continual unfolding of self-discovery and contribution to the world. It's about aligning your actions with your values, leveraging your unique gifts to make a positive impact and finding fulfilment in the meaningful connections forged along the way. As setbacks fade into the background, your purpose emerges as a guiding force, illuminating the path ahead and infusing each chapter of your life with purposeful meaning.

Pursuing God's purpose for your life adds a spiritual dimension to the journey of self-discovery. It involves seeking alignment with Divine guidance and surrendering to a higher calling. Amid setbacks, this pursuit takes on a profound significance, as it becomes a journey not just of personal fulfilment but of fulfilling the purpose that God has ordained.

Begin by cultivating a relationship with God through prayer, meditation and reflection. In moments of stillness, allow your heart to open to the whispers of Divine guidance. Seek clarity on how your unique gifts and inclinations align with God's plan for you. Often, setbacks can catalyse a deeper connection with the Divine, as they prompt a reassessment of priorities and a reliance on spiritual strength.

The Bible teaches that God has plans for each of us, plans for welfare and not for evil, to give us a future and hope (Jeremiah 29:11). Understanding and embracing this truth can provide comfort and direction, especially in the face of adversity. Your setbacks may be part of a larger narrative written by the hand of a loving Creator, shaping you for a purpose beyond your current understanding.

As you navigate life's challenges, consider the biblical concept of stewardship. It involves recognising that your life, including your talents, time and resources, is a gift entrusted to you by God. This awareness transforms the pursuit of purpose into a sacred responsibility – a commitment to use your God-given abilities to serve others and contribute positively to the world.

In pursuing God's purpose, patience and faith play pivotal roles. Setbacks may test your resolve, but faith encourages you to trust in God's timing and Divine plan. Even when the path seems unclear, your faith becomes a guiding light, illuminating the way forward.

Surround yourself with a supportive community of fellow believers who can encourage, share wisdom and pray alongside you. Seeking guidance from spiritual mentors or leaders can also be instrumental in discerning God's purpose for your life.

Remember that the pursuit of God's purpose is not separate from the practical aspects of daily living. It involves aligning your actions and decisions with the principles and values found in Scripture. Whether in your relationships, career or personal endeavours, strive to live by the teachings of love, compassion and justice.

Ultimately, pursuing God's purpose for your life is a dynamic, ongoing process. It's about walking hand in hand with the Divine, allowing your faith to guide your steps, and recognising that setbacks, though challenging, can be opportunities for spiritual growth and a deeper understanding of God's purpose in your life. As you continue on this sacred journey, may you find strength, peace, and fulfilment in the knowledge that you are living out the purpose for which you were uniquely created.

Has my way of life changed since my diagnosis? I say "yes," because now more than ever, I know that my journey through this earth is for a purpose. Heck, no I don't want to die full! The goal is to die empty, fulfilling all that I have been mandated to do by God. I live my life knowing each day is a gift for which I am thankful.

EMPOWERING THE ONE IN EIGHT

Chapter 7
Providing Essential Support

I realised that we as individuals always have high expectations of people – sometimes we expect so much. But what if we are expecting people to give what they don't have? In my moments of fear and anxiety, I was craving a relationship that did not exist and I was looking for someone to take the burden away. In my little bubble, I felt there must be somebody out there who could understand what I was going through one hundred per cent – someone who could completely take away the pain, the anxiety, the sadness and the hurt that I felt. Oh was I disappointed in the fact that I thought another human could! I soon realised not even my husband could. How dare I expect him to? He was also going through his anxiety and disappointment. I recall one of the days we lay in bed talking about my fears and anxieties, and I was so upset that the tears came flooding. I looked up only to realise that my husband was in tears and there and then I made the decision to speak positive words. I never wanted to see him in such a vulnerable state again.

When we go through setbacks, it is not the weight of the trials or adversity that determines our path, but how we leverage the support of those who surround us during these times. Support networks include families, peers and counsellors, who are made up of individuals who offer a variety of comfort and aid.

Family members who have a close intimate knowledge of our history often provide a comforting embrace, however, some might find it difficult when trying to offer objective support due to their emotional involvement. Accepting help or support from people is an art in itself, knowing that it is OK to be vulnerable; being mindful that when we draw strength from others, each person has a capacity and occasionally roles are reversed. In times of adversity, the support from those around us can make all the difference. This chapter explores the crucial role of providing essential support during difficult times, offering insights and strategies for effectively aiding others through life's storms.

Understanding the Need

Before delving into how to provide support, it's essential to understand the nature of the need. Difficult times can manifest in various forms, including loss, illness, financial struggles or mental health challenges. Recognising the unique circumstances of each individual allows for tailored and meaningful support.

Empathy and Active Listening

Empathy forms the cornerstone of effective support. By putting ourselves in another's shoes, we can better understand their emotions and experiences. Active listening, free of judgment or interruption, fosters a safe space for individuals to express their feelings and concerns openly.

Practical Assistance

Offering practical assistance can alleviate some of the burdens faced during difficult times. Whether it's helping with daily chores, providing meals, or offering transportation, tangible support can ease the load and demonstrate care and solidarity.

Emotional Support

Emotional support is equally vital: offering comfort, reassurance and companionship. Simply being present for someone, offering a listening ear, or sharing words of encouragement can provide immense comfort during challenging moments.

Respecting Boundaries

While support is essential, it's crucial to respect boundaries and individual preferences. Some individuals may prefer solitude or have specific needs regarding the type or frequency of support they receive. Respecting these boundaries honours their autonomy and fosters trust in the support relationship.

Maintaining Communication

Consistent communication is key to providing ongoing support. Check in regularly with those facing difficulties, offering continued encouragement and assistance as needed. Showing that you're there for the long haul reinforces the strength of your support network.

Self-Care for Supporters

Providing support during difficult times can be emotionally taxing. Supporters need to prioritise self-care, setting boundaries, seeking support from others when needed, and engaging in activities that recharge their emotional reserves.

In times of adversity, the support we provide to one another can serve as a lifeline, offering comfort, strength and hope. By understanding the needs of those facing difficulties and offering empathetic, practical and respectful support, we can navigate life's storms together, emerging stronger and more resilient than before.

Chapter 8
Confronting Your Fears

Before my diagnosis, I had a friend who had been diagnosed with breast cancer a few years back. I remember going to see my doctor a few days later and telling her that I just wanted to have a breast check. She did check and felt nothing. She asked at that time if I wanted to have a breast scan. For some reason, I said no. Now I know that it probably wasn't the right time and when it was, everything aligned.

A day before my operation I was so nervous because I had never been put to sleep for an operation. This was going to be my first surgery, so I was anxious. That evening, I had my close friends around and we prayed after the prayer and time spent together. I felt encouraged and at peace within. The next day I was up early, the kids were off to school and hubby had taken the day off to be with me. We arrived at the hospital, I changed into the gown and had to have a quick scan for the site to be marked. As we waited, I spent time praying and just believing God that this would be the first and the last operation I would have regarding this situation and my health in general. I was wheeled down to the scanning department. Just being in the breast scanning department brought back all the emotions that I had tried to hold back, and all of a sudden the floodgates opened I cried and cried. The poor lady who was supposed to do the scan kept on reassuring me and then she whispered, "God is in control." At that moment, I started to pull myself together. I had the Madonna bra attached (just a paper cup that holds the area marked and pinned together. So as soon as we got back, it was time to head into the operating room. I spoke to all my siblings and my parents that morning, we prayed together and gave Solomon one last hug and then I was wheeled in.

Getting into the operating room, the Anaesthetist got to work, reassuring me and telling me what was going to happen. He put an oxygen mask over my face and kept on telling me to breathe and relax and let myself go, but I wasn't prepared to fall asleep I wanted to stay awake as much as possible. My friends had shared how some of them had stayed awake during procedures they had and had heard ongoing conversations in the operating room. So, he could tell I was fighting to stay awake and then started to reassure me to let myself go and sleep, and that was all I remembered. The next time was me trying to wake up and someone was standing over me asking if I was OK. I opened my eyes. The first place my hand went to was my breast. It was still in place. I looked around and realised I was in the recovery unit. It all went well to the glory of God. I got home that same day to flowers, fruits and food from friends. I felt little or no pain after the spinal wore off. I did not have to take the pain relief I was given.

I remember going for a walk at home. I came across one of the nurses whom I had seen earlier during my booking appointment for the surgery. I brought my son to football practice in the park so I was just walking around the field. She called out to me, saying, "Why do you look sad?" I told her I had the surgery and was waiting to start my radiation therapy. She went ahead and told me off for walking around like I was carrying the whole world on my shoulders. She reminded me that what I had was zero stage and that there were people who had a far worse prognosis than I did. She encouraged me to celebrate life rather than act as if my life was over.

Before commencing my radiation therapy, I had to be measured and fitted and they had to decide the right position for me to be placed in, to avoid the radiation beam from going elsewhere. I remember feeling so vulnerable the first time, and all up in my feelings. And some days later I had a light bulb moment that indeed my breast size had sort of saved my life. You see, from a young age my breasts had stood out, and who knows whether the cancer may not have spread quicker if my breast size was smaller. Rather than being in an upright position and being at risk of radiation beams on the chest, I was placed lying face down and although it was the most uncomfortable, claustrophobic position, I believe it saved me in the long run. I attended my appointments by myself by choice. The first day, I cried coming in, I cried sitting and waiting for my turn, I cried changing. I took some selfies for reflection and cried whilst the radiation was ongoing. The technician must have heard me sobbing because when I was changed and ready to go home, he asked me if I had any songs that I wanted to play in the background while receiving the treatment. I was shocked. I couldn't believe the beautiful team who worked in the department were all Muslims and Saudis but they were so kind and thoughtful. They always had the right words to say, they always had a reassuring smile on their faces. It was as if they could read my mind and embodied the outward reaction. So I told him that I would come with a playlist the next day.

The next day as I sat waiting for my turn, he asked for my playlist and I gave it, most of the songs were by an artist called "Jonathan Traylor" and as I walked into the room, the song "I Trust You" echoed loud round the whole room. Although I had been listening to his songs for a while, at that present moment it was as if it was the first time I heard the song. I felt a warm sensation and God's presence right there in the room. I felt His embrace and of course, I was a sobbing mess, but it helped. At that moment, I said, "Thank you Lord for the Kingdom of Saudi Arabia. Thank you Lord for the people of this great nation and thank you Lord for being at the right place at the right time." Throughout my treatment, I would always walk in with Gospel songs playing in the background and it was confirmation that my healing had already taken place, and this process was just completing what God had already done.

One of the technicians approached me and said to me that she now plays the song over and over again as she loves the lyrics of the songs. I smiled because not only was God working on me in that room, but He was also working on the people around that environment.

Being in Saudi is a whole story on its own. Having lived out here for over eight years, it's amazing to see the dedication to their culture and beliefs and the dedication to their prayer times. I said to myself as a Christian if I took my prayer life as seriously as they do, the devil would be in trouble and indeed my prayer life has been up since moving to Saudi.

Being open, honest and authentic about one's vulnerability can be a source of strength and empowerment. Being vulnerable has never been something I found easy. My walk through this journey has indeed brought out my vulnerable side, showing the power that lies within. Sharing my story with friends or colleagues has fostered some deeper connections with others – encouraging others to reciprocate and share issues they have dealt with or are dealing with.

Telling my story was indeed something that I had to do. I know that it required courage, it had to involve being judged or rejected by some. However, it helped build my resilience. I wanted to let people know what type of support can be given to people going through challenges. The power of vulnerability lies in the ability to strengthen connection, foster personal and collective growth and create a more compassionate and authentic way of engaging with oneself and others. I remember trying to do some research on social media after my diagnosis. I was overwhelmed at seeing the number of young people battling with this – people in their late twenties! Gone are the days when breast cancer was linked to older women and now it is very common amongst young people. I couldn't wait for the hospital to do a genetic test, so I went ahead and got one done privately before my operation. I wanted to know what the best decision was. So, I went out of KSA to have it done and thankfully the result was negative meaning that I don't carry the gene. I also repeated it when the hospital and the result was the same. I decided that breast cancer was not going to have the best of me, but that I was going to use this God-given opportunity to empower myself and others. Owning my narrative of this diagnosis was important and seeing God's hands in all of this. Lifelong lessons came with this setback and brought with it valuable lessons. Each challenge was an opportunity to strengthen my resilience which allowed me to bounce back stronger than before. I had faced some health scares in the past, but I did not know the strength I carried. The Holy Spirit was at work daily helping me draw strength from within. There are so many negative stories on social media and although they were positives, I realised that each person's journey is personal to them – two people don't go through the same thing.

Rising Strong: Finding Strength and Empowerment Through Life's Challenges

Can one ever be empowered if they have never dealt with or faced challenges? You cannot grow from what you have not been through. Admitting that this stage of my life was indeed a challenge, for a while I could not see the light at the end of the tunnel. I was getting myself in – it felt like I kept on falling. Until I admitted that it was beyond my comprehension and laid it down at His feet, that was when help came.

Yes, it is easy to say, "Oh you didn't have cancer! According to Google's description, cancer is something that has spread and yours did not." Being diagnosed in the first place, was something I never expected. It was like dealing with grief somewhat: The old me was gone and my life at that moment changed forever. I miss the carefree person that I was to an extent; I had no worries in the world. I would Netflix and chill and lie in for as long as I wanted. Yes, I had goals and ambitions but I did not put a timeline on those. I did not have the burning desire that I have now to make each moment count, and I was not intentional about certain things. Yes, I feel like the diagnosis threw me a lifeline and every second counts for me. I am eager to see the visions and dreams given to me come to pass. Spending quality time with the ones I love, being physically present in the now, rather than planning a future that might not exist, I don't know what tomorrow holds but I know the One who holds tomorrow. I run with the vision, I live a life of purpose, my goals have indeed changed, and the way I view life has changed.

In everything give thanks. I give thanks for this season of my life, because if not for God it would have been a different story. You have to look for the silver lining and grow from experience. Somebody once asked if I feel disappointed having served and believed God. Why would He allow such challenges? I responded by saying that nowhere in the Bible it mentions a life free from challenges. Rather, He has given us all we need to overcome.

Many are the afflictions of the righteous, but the Lord delivers us from them all (Psalm 34:19).

The Power of Praise and Worship

Playing Gospel songs during trying times can have a profound impact on individuals, offering emotional, spiritual, and psychological support. Here are some ways in which Gospel music can positively influence individuals facing challenges:

1. Comfort and Encouragement

   Gospel songs often contain messages of hope, comfort and encouragement. The lyrics may remind individuals of God's love, faithfulness and the promise of better days. This can provide solace during difficult moments and inspire a sense of perseverance.

2. Expression of Faith

   Gospel music allows individuals to express their faith and trust in God even when facing adversity. Singing or listening to songs that proclaim God's sovereignty and goodness can reinforce one's connection to their faith and help maintain a positive perspective.

3. Spiritual Upliftment

   The uplifting melodies and powerful lyrics of gospel songs can have a spiritual impact, lifting the spirits of those going through challenging times. Music can touch the soul, providing a sense of peace and connection to the Divine.

4. Promotion of Reflection and Prayer

   Gospel songs often encourage reflection on one's faith and a deepening of the prayer life. The act of listening to or singing Gospel music can create a meditative atmosphere, allowing individuals to connect with God through prayer and contemplation.

5. Sense of Community

    Gospel music is often associated with communal worship. Listening to gospel songs can evoke a sense of community and shared faith, even when individuals are physically alone. This sense of connection with a broader faith community can be reassuring during trying times.

6. Positive Impact on Mood

    Music has the power to influence mood and emotions. Gospel songs, with their uplifting and joyous nature, can positively impact one's mood, fostering a more optimistic outlook despite challenging circumstances.

7. Reminders of God's Promises

    Gospel lyrics often include references to biblical promises and assurances. Hearing these reminders, especially during difficult times, can reinforce the belief that God is faithful and can be relied upon for strength and guidance.

8. Cathartic Release

    Music, including Gospel songs, can provide a cathartic release for emotions. Singing along or simply listening to expressive lyrics can be a way to process feelings of sadness, frustration, or anxiety, offering a healthy emotional outlet.

9. Fostering Resilience

    The themes of overcoming trials, finding strength in God, and experiencing transformation are common in gospel music. These messages can contribute to the development of resilience, helping individuals navigate challenges with faith and perseverance.

10. Promotion of Gratitude

Some Gospel songs focus on gratitude and thanksgiving, even amid difficulties. Practising gratitude is linked to improved mental well-being and can provide a more balanced perspective during trying times.

In summary, playing Gospel songs during challenging moments can be a source of strength, encouragement and spiritual connection. The combination of uplifting melodies and affirming lyrics creates an atmosphere that fosters resilience and reinforces the hope that comes from faith.

Chapter 9
Christian Perspectives on Trials

The idea of trials and challenges is a recurring theme in Christian theology, often viewed through the lens of faith and spiritual growth. While different denominations and theological perspectives may interpret this concept in various ways, here are some common Christian perspectives on trials:

1. Biblical References

    Many passages in the Bible speak about facing trials and challenges. For example, James 1:2-4 (NIV) states, "Consider it pure joy, my brothers and sisters, whenever you face trials of many kinds because you know that the testing of your faith produces perseverance. Let perseverance finish its work so that you may be mature and complete, not lacking anything." These verses suggest that trials can be an essential part of spiritual development.

2. Refining Faith

    Some Christians believe that trials serve to refine and strengthen one's faith. Just as precious metals are purified through fire, believers may view challenges as opportunities for their faith to be refined and deepened. The process of facing difficulties and relying on God for strength can lead to spiritual growth.

3. Learning Trust and Dependency on God

Trials can teach believers to trust God more fully. When facing challenges, individuals often turn to their faith for guidance, strength and comfort. Experiencing dependence on God during difficult times can deepen one's relationship with the Divine.

4. Purpose in Adversity

    Christians may see purpose in adversity, believing that God can work through trials for the greater good. Romans 8:28 (NIV) expresses this sentiment: "And we know that in all things God works for the good of those who love Him, who have been called according to His purpose."

5. Empathy and Compassion

    Going through trials can also cultivate empathy and compassion in believers. Those who have faced challenges may be more understanding and supportive of others going through similar struggles, fulfilling the Christian call to love and care for one another.

6. Testimony of Faith

    Christians may see trials as an opportunity to bear witness to their faith. Enduring challenges with grace and trust in God's plan can serve as a testimony to the transformative power of faith.

It's important to note that individual interpretations of the role of trials in the Christian faith may vary. While some see trials as necessary for spiritual growth, others may view them as part of the complex nature of human existence. Additionally, Christians often turn to prayer, community support and reliance on their faith to navigate and overcome trials.

Confronting Your Fears: A Journey to Personal Empowerment

Fear is something we all deal with differently, it's an experience that can either leave us feeling numb or paralyzed or give us the boost we need to move forward. Fear can impact our lives I remember after my diagnosis wanting to just coil up and do nothing, I could not move past the word CANCER, I could not think or process my thoughts I just felt numb. Receiving a diagnosis can be a life-altering moment that brings a flood of emotions and uncertainties. It was not unit I began the journey of confronting and overcoming it that I healed from that trauma. Yes, my diagnosis was a traumatic event in my life, and it took me writing this book to understand that one has to understand the emotional impact of a diagnosis to be able to begin the process of confronting fear. I remember in the different vulnerable moments that I experienced a scripture came to mind, Psalms 23:4 Even though I walk through the darkest valley I will fear no evil for you are with me your rod and your staff they comfort me. Joshua 1:19 Have I not commanded you? Be strong and courageous. Do not be afraid do not be discouraged for the Lord your God will be with you wherever you go. The fear of not making it out was my biggest concern, I was scared of not being there for my children, what if the lumpectomy came back with a different report, I couldn't get past that thought. I looked at my children differently most times with guilt, that I might not get to see them reach certain milestones in life. I had to be very intentional in confronting my fears and this required resilience. Affirming that cancer was not my fault or anything that I did wrong

The Spectrum of Emotions

Fear is an emotion that we all get to experience at some point in our lives. Some of the emotions that stem from fear include anger, sadness, denial and acceptance. I remember after my diagnosis feeling so angry and disappointed after my dedication and trying to live a godly life. I did not deserve what was happening to me: This definitely wasn't God's promise for my life; this wasn't the plan. I remember growing up and I will always hear people use the phrase "it is not my portion" and I will always wonder whose portion it was! For days I sat wondering why this was happening to me, I couldn't see beyond that question. I felt so depressed and sad – indeed if we allow fear, it takes complete hold of our senses. I did not want to speak to anyone, during the early days Solomon would try to encourage me through scriptures but I just didn't want to hear it, I just wanted to be left alone, I prayed to wake up the next day and be told it was all a dream and be back to my life, but atlas this was my reality, it was happening I was in the biggest fight of my life mentally and physically. I felt somebody was trying to pull the rug from under my feet, I was not going to let the devil have the last laugh, no I had not come this far in faith to let the devil win. "No!" I screamed and I declared, "Greater is He that is in me than he that is in the world." Since I was born and from my early days of understanding who God is, He has always come through for me and my family, the testimonies that I have experienced in my lifetime are enough to know that the "I am that I am" was not going to leave or forsake me. So as I began to understand these emotions I began to speak directly to each one. Only once I began to do that, that was when the relief came, that was when the burden began to fall off.

"The Lord is my light and my salvation whom shall I fear? The Lord is the stronghold of my life of whom shall I be afraid." – Psalm 27:1

The Challenges of Post-Diagnosis Fear

I did not want the attention that came with a diagnosis like mine, so only a few people knew and my family. Being very reserved, the last thing I wanted was for everyone to feel sorry for me and the stigma associated with it. So throughout my appointments, apart from the first day of radiation therapy, I went alone, because I could be myself and cry without reservations. I also did not want to put my friends under pressure by always checking on me. However, that did not stop me from having certain expectations of what I felt my friends should be doing. It was a prayer point because I felt that the support that I truly needed was not there. I understood why sometimes people do not share their problems with friends because they don't want to feel like a burden. Support networks are important during difficult times – it helps to navigate the challenges ahead.

Chapter 10
Navigating Breast Cancer Treatment and Lifestyle Changes

Introduction

A breast cancer diagnosis can be overwhelming, but understanding and navigating the treatment process is crucial for achieving the best possible outcomes. This chapter guides comprehending breast cancer treatment plans and incorporating lifestyle changes to support overall well-being during this challenging journey.

Understanding Your Breast Cancer Treatment Plan

Upon receiving a breast cancer diagnosis, it's essential to engage in open communication with your healthcare team. I had an advantage because I was a health care professional, although this was a different field compared to what I do, I understood my care plan and also spoke up with decisions that I was not happy with. Gain a thorough understanding of your treatment plan, including surgery, chemotherapy, radiation therapy, hormone therapy, or a combination thereof. Ask questions about potential side effects, treatment duration, and the expected outcomes. This knowledge empowers you to actively participate in decision-making and feel more in control of your health.

Building a Support System

Facing breast cancer requires a strong support system, you cannot deal with all the emotions alone, so having somebody to talk to and share your concerns and worries with is always helpful. But one thing I learnt is that you have to be ready to share and to be vulnerable to Share your concerns, fears, and triumphs with friends, family, and healthcare professionals. Their encouragement and assistance can provide emotional support, helping you cope with the challenges of treatment.

Adopting Healthy Lifestyle Changes

In parallel with medical treatments, embracing healthy lifestyle changes is crucial for managing the physical and emotional toll of breast cancer. Nutrition plays a pivotal role in supporting your body during treatment. Consult a nutritionist to develop a tailored plan that addresses your unique needs. A diet rich in antioxidants, lean proteins, and essential nutrients can aid in recovery and improve overall well-being.

Physical activity is beneficial during breast cancer treatment. Engage in activities that suit your fitness levels, such as walking, gentle yoga, or swimming. Regular exercise not only improves physical strength but also contributes to emotional well-being, reducing stress and anxiety.

Coping with Lifestyle Changes

Adjusting to new lifestyle habits can be challenging. Address emotional and psychological barriers by seeking support from mental health professionals, joining support groups, or practising mindfulness. Acknowledge and process your emotions, allowing yourself the space to grieve and celebrate victories, no matter how small.

Setting Realistic Goals

Establish realistic goals to maintain motivation and a positive outlook. Break down long-term objectives into manageable steps. Celebrate each achievement, such as completing a treatment phase or managing side effects effectively. Setting and accomplishing smaller goals contribute to a sense of control and empowerment.

Embracing a Positive Mindset

Maintaining a positive mindset is crucial throughout breast cancer treatment. Focus on the present, practice gratitude, and visualize a healthier future. Surround yourself with positivity and engage in activities that bring joy and fulfilment, contributing to an overall sense of well-being.

IFY OJI

Chapter 11
Conclusion

Navigating breast cancer treatment involves a combination of medical interventions and lifestyle adjustments. By understanding your treatment plan, building a strong support system, adopting healthy lifestyle changes, and cultivating a positive mindset, you can enhance your physical and emotional well-being. Remember, each step forward brings you closer to healing and a future of renewed health and vitality.

We are grateful that the cancer was caught early and it was ductal carcinoma (which is zero stage), but treatment decisions had to be made and I wanted to do a genetic test to decide what mode of treatment would be suitable. Thankfully, the result from the genetic test was negative. I remember feeling anxious about this so I had to have a lumpectomy which was an operation to remove the lump. This surgery was the first surgery apart from a caesarean section (that I had to deliver my twins). This was the first time that I was going to have general anaesthesia. I was petrified and began to focus on all that could go wrong. Also, another biopsy would be done on the lump that was removed and if they did not succeed in removing all the parts of the lump, another surgery would be done. By God's grace, the surgery was a success and the test from the lump was the same with some parts being benign. This meant that I did not have to go through chemotherapy and I only needed radiotherapy which also came with certain side effects. However, all things worked together and I had very minimal burns and no major side effects.

Shifting Perspective: From Victim to Survivor

Once I had gone through all the emotions, only then was I able to focus on the miracle that I had just experienced, from a God-ordained conversation with a real-life angel to having a USS. This all happened before my fortieth birthday which would have been when I was legible for a mammogram. I mean I felt nothing, apart from some aches during my period I did not have any other issues. It all started from a moment of sincere prayer – indeed He is a God who hears and meets us at the point of our needs. I started thanking and worshipping God and I lay it all down at His feet. That was when my mentality changed. I knew the battle was already won at this point. I remember the breast surgeon was so sure that it was nothing and told me several times that I did not need to have a biopsy. But I was adamant and kept on requesting for one and I am thankful that I remained sensitive to the Holy Spirit. Up until this day, I have shivers down my spine, with how everything turned out for my good.

Through this phase studying the Word of God brought me peace. I felt at ease, yet my emotions fluctuated through the days: some days were made up of waking up and going for my appointment (seeing as most of the patients in the oncology department were all elderly, I saw very few young faces). Then came the self-pity. Those days were spent in my room post-treatment with Gospel music playing in the background until I slept it off. The evenings were spent walking. I loved walking but during this period it was my escape – it was where I just let myself go. I recall taking one of the twins for soccer and I met a lady whom I had previously seen at the hospital.

"For I am convinced that neither death nor life, neither angels nor demons, neither the present nor the future, nor any powers, neither height nor depth, nor anything else in all creation, will be able to separate us from the love of God that is in Christ Jesus." – Romans 8:38, 39

Living in a relaxed environment while dealing with a diagnosis – especially a challenging one such as breast cancer – can have profound effects on both physical and mental well-being. I am blessed to be in a country where I did not have to be kept on the waiting list and where the latest treatment plan is offered free of charge. I remember telling someone that I was not too sure the story would have been the same if I was still back in the United Kingdom, as if an early detection would have happened.

Here are some positive impacts:

1. Reduced Stress Levels

    A relaxed environment can significantly contribute to lowering stress levels. Chronic stress is known to adversely affect health, especially during a medical challenge like breast cancer. Creating a calm and peaceful space can promote a sense of tranquillity, helping to alleviate stress and anxiety.

2. Enhanced Emotional Well-being

    Living in a relaxed setting provides a conducive space for emotional healing. It allows individuals to process their emotions — from fear and sadness to hope and gratitude. Emotional well-being is crucial in coping with the challenges of a diagnosis and undergoing treatment.

3. Improved Sleep Quality

   A relaxed environment supports better sleep quality. Quality sleep is essential for the body's healing processes, and individuals dealing with a diagnosis often face disruptions in their sleep patterns. A comfortable and soothing environment can contribute to better sleep, promoting overall recovery.

4. Positive Impact on Physical Health

   Stress reduction and improved emotional well-being can have a positive impact on physical health. The body's ability to cope with the challenges of treatment, recover from surgeries, and respond to medications can be influenced by the overall state of well-being.

5. Enhanced Decision-Making

   A relaxed environment fosters clarity of thought and improved decision-making. Individuals can better focus on understanding their diagnosis and treatment options, and making informed choices when they are not overwhelmed by stress or external pressures.

6. Supportive Relationships

   A relaxed environment often encourages the development and maintenance of supportive relationships. Family and friends may feel more comfortable providing assistance and emotional support when the atmosphere is conducive to open communication and understanding.

7. Encouraging Healthy Lifestyle Choices

    Living in a relaxed environment supports the adoption of healthy lifestyle choices. It becomes easier to maintain a balanced diet, engage in regular physical activity, and adhere to treatment plans when stressors are minimized.

8. Fostering a Positive Mindset

    A relaxed environment contributes to the cultivation of a positive mindset. Positivity can play a vital role in the healing process, influencing the overall experience of the diagnosis and treatment.

9. Promoting Mind-Body Connection

    A relaxed environment encourages individuals to engage in activities that promote the mind-body connection, such as meditation, deep breathing exercises, or yoga. These practices can have holistic benefits for physical and mental well-being.

10. Increasing Resilience

    Living in a relaxed environment fosters resilience, and the ability to bounce back from challenges. Resilience is a valuable asset when navigating the complexities of a medical diagnosis and treatment, contributing to a more optimistic outlook on the future. I was so blessed to have work colleagues who understood that I did not want the attention and treated me as normal. I was offered light duties for a while at work. My work pattern changed once I returned to work. I am blessed to still be able to do a job that I love, and I remain thankful. We need to change our perspective when it comes to hospitals. We need to start seeing the hospital as a place where healthy people go and that way we stay on top of early diagnosis and treatment.

In conclusion, creating a relaxed environment can positively impact the experience of dealing with a diagnosis like breast cancer. It provides a foundation for emotional and physical well-being, facilitating a more holistic and positive approach to the challenges of diagnosis and treatment.

The Bible contains various passages that emphasise the importance of offering emotional support and comfort to others. Here are a few verses that convey this message:

1. 2 Corinthians 1:3-4 (NIV)

   "Praise be to the God and Father of our Lord Jesus Christ, the Father of compassion and the God of all comfort, who comforts us in all our troubles so that we can comfort those in any trouble with the comfort we receive."

2. Galatians 6:2 (NIV)

   "Carry each other's burdens, and in this way, you will fulfil the law of Christ."

3. Proverbs 17:17 (NIV)

   "A friend loves at all times, and a brother is born for a time of adversity."

4. Romans 12:15 (NIV)

   "Rejoice with those who rejoice; mourn with those who mourn."

5. 1 Thessalonians 5:11 (NIV)

   "Therefore encourage one another and build each other up, just as in fact, you are doing."

6. Isaiah 41:10 (NIV)

   "So do not fear, for I am with you; do not be dismayed, for I am your God. I will strengthen you and help you; I will uphold you with My righteous right hand."

7. Psalm 34:18 (NIV)

   "The Lord is close to the broken-hearted and saves those who are crushed in spirit."

8. Matthew 5:4 (NIV)

   "Blessed are those who mourn, for they will be comforted."

9. Colossians 3:12-14 (NIV)

   "Therefore, as God's chosen people, holy and dearly loved, clothe yourselves with compassion, kindness, humility, gentleness, and patience. Bear with each other and forgive one another if any of you has a grievance against someone. Forgive as the Lord forgave you. And over all these virtues, put on love, which binds them all together in perfect unity."

10. Hebrews 10:24-25 (NIV)

"And let us consider how we may spur one another on toward love and good deeds, not giving up meeting together, as some are in the habit of doing, but encouraging one another – and all the more as you see the Day approaching."

These verses emphasise the Christian principles of compassion, empathy, and support for others, particularly during times of difficulty or distress. They encourage believers to be a source of comfort and encouragement to those in need, reflecting the love and compassion of God.

Facing a life-changing diagnosis can be an overwhelming and challenging experience. Many turn to their faith to find meaning and solace during such times. The concept of God's plan for one's life becomes a source of comfort and guidance. Here are some perspectives from the Bible on trusting in God's plan:

1. Jeremiah 29:11 (NIV)

"For I know the plans I have for you, declares the Lord, plans for welfare and not for evil, to give you a future and a hope."

This verse is often quoted to emphasise that God has a purpose and plan for each person, even amid challenges.

2. Romans 8:28 (NIV)

"And we know that in all things God works for the good of those who love him, who have been called according to His purpose."

This passage reassures believers that God is working for their good, even in the face of adversity.

3. Proverbs 3:5-6 (NIV)

    "Trust in the Lord with all your heart and lean not on your understanding; in all your ways submit to Him, and He will make your paths straight."

    Trusting in God's plan involves surrendering to His wisdom and guidance, even when life takes unexpected turns.

4. Isaiah 41:10 (NIV)

    "So do not fear, for I am with you; do not be dismayed, for I am your God. I will strengthen you and help you; I will uphold you with My righteous right hand."

    God's promise to be with you during challenging times reinforces the belief that His plan includes providing strength and support.

5. Psalm 139:16 (NIV)

    "Your eyes saw my unformed body; all the days ordained for me were written in your book before one of them came to be."

This verse reflects the idea that God has ordained every day of our lives, and nothing takes Him by surprise.

6. Philippians 4:6-7 (NIV)

    "Do not be anxious about anything, but in every situation, by prayer and petition, with thanksgiving, present your requests to God. And the peace of God, which transcends all understanding, will guard your hearts and your minds in Christ Jesus."

    Trusting in God's plan involves seeking His guidance through prayer and finding peace in His sovereignty.

7. Romans 12:2 (NIV)

    "Do not conform to the pattern of this world but be transformed by the renewing of your mind. Then you will be able to test and approve what God's will is – His good, pleasing, and perfect will."

    Trusting in God's plan may require a shift in perspective, aligning one's understanding with His Divine will.

8. 2 Corinthians 4:17 (NIV)

    "For our light and momentary troubles are achieving for us an eternal glory that far outweighs them all."

    This verse encourages believers to view difficulties as temporary in the grander scope of God's eternal plan.

During a life-changing diagnosis, holding on to these biblical perspectives can offer a foundation of hope, peace and assurance in God's plan: It provides a lens through which individuals can navigate their journey with faith and resilience.

One out of eight women is at risk of developing breast cancer once in their lifetime, according to the World Health Organisation (WHO). It is a disease which results in abnormal breast cells growing out of control and forming tumours. If left unchecked, the tumours spread throughout the body and become fatal. Breast cancer cells begin inside the milk ducts – the earliest form which – in situ – is not seen as life-threatening. Cancer cells can spread into nearby breast tissues which is called invasion. Treatments vary and are based on the individual, the type of cancer and its spread. Treatments combine surgery, radiation therapy and medication.

Whilst doing my research online it was evident that, over the past few decades, there has been an observed increase in the incidence of breast cancer in younger women. While breast cancer is more common in older age groups, cases among women under forty have been on the rise (WHO, 2022).

Several factors might contribute to the rise in breast cancer diagnoses among young people, including lifestyle changes, reproductive patterns, delayed childbirth, use of hormonal contraceptives and environmental factors. Additionally, advances in early detection methods may lead to more cases being identified in younger populations. In some cases, genetic factors, such as mutations in the BRCA1 and BRCA2 genes, can increase the risk of early-onset breast cancer. Genetic testing and increased awareness of hereditary factors have led to more early detections in younger individuals.

Hormonal influences, both endogenous and exogenous, are believed to play a role. Factors such as early puberty, late menopause and the use of hormonal therapies may contribute to an increased risk. Improved awareness about breast cancer symptoms, regular screening practices, and advancements in imaging technologies may lead to the identification of breast cancer cases at earlier stages, including in younger individuals.

Symptoms of breast cancer can include:

- A breast lump or thickening (often without pain),
- Change in size, shape and appearance of the breast,
- Dimpling, redness, pitting or other changes,
- Changes in nipple appearance,
- Abnormal body fluid from the nipple.

It is advisable to carry out frequent breast checks, to notice a deviation from the norm. It is important to note that most lumps are not cancer.

Summary

Every day, I stride confidently, shoulders squared, head held high. Yet, amidst whispers of relief, I ponder: Have we forsaken our duty as our brothers' keepers? Illness spares no one. Do you know anyone facing a setback or adversity? This is your opportunity to show empathy and offer support.

Irrespective of my journey through life, the past years have broadened my views. I no longer have the same views – I see life differently. Being able to reflect has given me all that I need to propel myself forward. The big views, goals and dreams no longer move me; it's the little things that count. I am more intentional about being present now, thankful for each moment I get to be present. I have been thrown a lifeline and to that, I owe myself some grace and I vowed to be more intentional with the people I love and care about and be the best version of myself with people that I come across daily.

When faced with a life-altering diagnosis, it is important to understand the cycle of emotions that one has to go through during this phase. Having a reflective attitude propels you forward in so many meaningful ways, that we develop as learners and as people without criticising. If I know the One who holds tomorrow, the One who created the universe, the One who decrees a thing and it comes to pass, I have no reason to worry about tomorrow. We walk by faith and not by sight. We serve a living God who knows the end from the beginning. We always have to remind ourselves of the significance of the things we go through as individuals and make a conscious effort to always look at the bigger picture. My story could have been different but Mercy said no.

Setbacks and adversities have a way of propelling you to the next level. Before my diagnosis, I was doing just OK. Now I want to run with the vision – with purpose – because now I have an understanding of the time.

"When I was a child, I spoke as a child, I understood as a child, I thought or reasoned as a child but when I became a man, I put away childish things." – 1 Corinthians 13:11

This Bible passage resonates with me. Indeed, one cannot grow through what one hasn't been through.

We all need somebody to lean on during difficult times. I pray to be a better friend when I am needed, and I pray I can offer support to friends if and when the need arises. No man is an island – we need each other. Indeed a friend loves at all times, and a brother is born for a time of adversity.

God has not given us the spirit of fear but of wisdom and sound mind. I once read somewhere that fear is faith reversed. The Bible admonishes us as Christians to be anxious about nothing, but by prayer and supplications to make our request known to God. This is what I did; putting every doubt and anxiety aside and offering praise and worship to the Father.

Amid life's storms, find your peace in the anchor of Christ Jesus, for His love is the calm that stills every troubled heart and the strength that carries us through every trial.

Sources

Giaquinto AN, Sung H, Miller KD, Kramer JL, Newman LA, Minihan A, Jemal A, Siegel RL. Breast Cancer Statistics, 2022. CA Cancer J Clin. 2022 Nov;72(6):524-541. doi: 10.3322/caac.21754. Epub 2022 Oct 3. PMID: 36190501.

EMPOWERING THE ONE IN EIGHT

About the Author

Ify Oji is a seasoned healthcare professional with nearly two decades of expertise in nursing and midwifery. Beyond her career, she enjoys reading, hiking and dancing. She passionately dedicates her time to supporting and coaching women to reach their full potential, embodying a commitment to personal growth and empowerment.

About PublishU

PublishU is transforming the world of publishing.

PublishU has developed a new and unique approach to publishing books, offering a three-step guided journey to becoming a globally published author!

We enable hundreds of people a year to write their book within 100-days, publish their book in 100-days and launch their book over 100-days to impact tens of thousands of people worldwide.

The journey is transformative, one author said,

"I never thought I would be able to write a book, let alone in 100 days... now I'm asking myself what else have I told myself that can't be done that actually can?'"

To find out more visit
www.PublishU.com

EMPOWERING THE ONE IN EIGHT

Printed in Great Britain
by Amazon